MW01269294

Wisdom Warriors

Mary Cole Watson, M. Ed.

"All children are beautiful, gifted,
unique and special.

When they believe this of themselves
they will become their best selves."

MARY COLE WATSON, M. Ed. ©

Dedication

To my ancestors and all African American youth.

A Special ██████████

Thanks

People are never successful by themselves. There are always supporters who help us navigate and fulfill our goals in life. So, I would like to first thank my husband, Marvin, who has always wholeheartedly supported all of my endeavors. I love him dearly for loving me unconditionally. He is an exceptional father with a confident, loving, humorous, and peaceful personality. I would also like to thank my three adult children whose childhood experiences provided me with material that make up these stories. Our firstborn, Marvin, academically gifted, cerebral, athletic, charismatic, and a compassionate child. Melissa, academically gifted, cerebral, shy, and a phenomenal writer and artist. Miranda, my youngest, academically gifted, athletic, inquisitive, and very humorous. She marched to the beat of a different drummer.

Gerard, my younger sibling, was an invaluable resource throughout the writing of my book. He is an astute businessman and manager of celebrity talent.

I was ecstatic that he took a deep interest in my book. Gerard guided me throughout the process with constructive comments, recommendations, and promotion of my book. He led me to Michelle Gines, Thaddeus Jordan, and Valerie Johnson. Their assistance led to additional story ideas, cover illustration, and invaluable feedback on storytelling. Gerard's impeccable negotiation skill, humor, positivity, and the immense knowledge he brings to any project he undertakes, made the publishing of this book a reality and a dream come true.

Taking a job in Cleveland Heights, Ohio, after obtaining my Masters from Toledo University, was one of my best life decisions. My Cleveland family has been a very close adopted extended family. Pamela Davis, and her entire family, have adopted me as their own within the first few months of my arrival to Cleveland. Jamie Mulazim and Pat Williams, became some of my closest friends. Claude and Tensie Holland, and Sylvia Stewart- Lumpkin, have encouraged me to write. Tensie was the person who convinced me to call *The New York Times* Best Selling author, Regina Brett, to share my *"Mission Statements for African American Youth."* Brett labeled them profound in our conversation and published the Mission Statements in a Sunday column of the *Plain Dealer.* Children's author, Tricia Springstubb, was the first person to read my manuscript, and encouraged me to publish my work.

I would also like to thank all of my students, especially students at Cleveland Heights High School where I taught for over two decades. So many dreams of working in a high school came to fruition for me at Heights High. We won state championships in my favorite sports of basketball and track and field. I was so honored to be one of many assistants for Heights Track and Field, coached by renowned Head Ohio Hall of Fame and National Track and Field Coach Claude Holland. Under his leadership, we captured the State Championship in 2008. Countless Heights High graduates have become national and world wide superstars in every conceivable prestigious career. Finally, I am thankful to Antoinette and Noel who credited me for their decision to become teachers.

I tried very hard not to have favorite students, because I remember that I didn't think it was fair for teachers to have favorites when I was a young child. So, I tried to like all of my students for their individual characteristics. I tried extra hard to like the challenging students, and even those who didn't like me. This wasn't as difficult to do as some people may think. I say this because the challenging students generally had abysmal living conditions, or maybe my teaching style didn't suit particular needs. Rather than dwell on offensive actions, I dwelled on self-reflection to see how I could reach those particular students. I felt it was my job as a teacher to instruct at a high level, and have a positive relationship with my students, so that they could focus on my expectations of them. When students know that you genuinely care for their well-being, the majority of the difficult ones will come around to become your biggest advocate. I love teaching and I love what students have taught me. I strongly believe that the teaching profession is best suited to be creative, compassionate, self- reflective individuals who have a genuine love for children of all cultures, and who view children as our most valuable resource.

Being human, I discovered that no matter how I tried to not have a favorite student, there is a student who impacted my life more than any other. I began to realize this fact when I was deciding on the few students and athletes that I would ask to say a few words about me at my retirement party. The first student I thought to invite was Jacques Evans. Jacques wasn't a great student because he didn't like to complete assignments, but his brilliance, charisma, zest for life, positive attitude, comedic acumen, and confidence were infectious. Jacques' personality was so endearing that when he was absent from class, he was sorely missed. When my husband reported to me that Jacques had informed him that he would be in New York City on business the date of my retirement party, I understood, but was crushed. My husband could not have done a better job organizing the party and the events. It was a memorable experience in every way, but there were moments during the evening when I thought of Jacques. I would come to find out that Jacques appreciated me as his teacher, as much as I appreciated teaching him on the night of his wedding rehearsal dinner. I was enjoying my meal and listening to Jacques express gratitude to deserving people, when suddenly I heard my name announced. Jacques presented me with a plaque as his favorite teacher. I was so overcome with emotion and gratitude that I was unable to express those feelings in words. That same year, Jacques was inducted into Heights Hall of Fame. He had already acknowledged his gratitude for me, so I was not expecting him to spend time during his speech to tell the audience why I was his favorite teacher. Jacques' demonstration of respect and gratitude for me rates among the most significant events in my life. Jacques is married to a stunning woman; whose external and inner beauty are quite captivating. Jacques is an exceptional father, and extremely successful businessman.

Everything that I do, is in honor of my ancestors, and so I end my acknowledgements with heartfelt gratitude for all that they have endured and sacrificed for the survival of future generations of African Americans.

Table of ▮▮▮▮▮▮
Contents

Overview ███████████████

Wisdom Warriors

Wisdom Warriors represents the very challenging conversations some African American parents have to have with their children. While the subjects are important for every family, these subjects tend to take on different characteristics when addressed from specific cultural and social points of view. Some parents are unsure of how to start the conversation, or to answer difficult questions in which children can understand fully, yet come away from the conversation feeling uplifted, rather than defeated by the unfair harsh realities of racism.

Wisdom Warriors is a series of short stories featuring Grandpa Marv, Grandma Mary, and Skye. Each story has been written as an interactive conversation within a loving family. Each story addresses specific, and difficult topics, in a way that all children, between the ages of nine to eighteen (adolescents to teenagers) can understand. The primary character, Skye, helps young readers understand the meaning of the problems they may experience through relatable activities, while weaving cultural facts and history to help the reader grasp value and pride in their own uniqueness. Instead of having children feel that something is "wrong" with them, readers will see their value through Skye and her grandparents', as wisdom warriors. The historical and foundational facts discussed throughout the series are designed to enlighten today's youth; that they are not at all responsible for the damaging, false beliefs of other

11

children or adults. In fact, it is the author's goal to equip each young reader with the knowledge to empower him, or her, to dispel the social stereotypes and rhetoric that often keeps him or her from reaching their full potential.

Grandpa Marv and Grandma Mary share their wisdom throughout this book, having experienced or witnessed some of problems that are dealt with in these short stories. Skye, Grandpa Marv, and Grandma Mary are entertaining characters that in a very practical way, demonstrate everyday life experiences, relationships, and challenges that arise as they go about their daily lives.

African American History has been woven into each story, to educate children and adults who are not familiar with the historical significance of the topics discussed. The stories are great for educators and all cultures because the wisdom shared serves as an education for everyone to understand the unique and troubling experiences of people of color.

I am what time, circumstance, history, have made of me, certainly, but I am also, much more than that. So are we all. James Baldwin

Preface

I was keenly aware of the world's injustice at a very young age because I was subjected to many types of bias as a child. Consequently, I was consumed with a longing need to escape an environment filled with experiences that wanted me to believe I was inferior to everyone else. With the passing of time, and my own personal victories, the wounds of these inequalities were all, but erased. However, as I emerged from my personal confinement of prejudice and self-hate, my eyes were opened to the conscious and unconscious suffocating grasp of racism on African Americans and other people of color.

The reality of racism was clearly defined for me around the age of six. No one had to point out the absence of African Americans and people of color, nor the subservient roles they played, as if they were present on TV. Even as a child, this fact truly depressed me. However, it never occurred to me that the absence of people of color on television was the result of having no access to such coveted roles due to racism. I remember thinking of how adults, who teach children to choose right over wrong, *choose* wrong on so many levels.

The adult response was often, "It isn't fair, but that's just the way it is." My thought was always to those answers was, "Yes, life is unfair, but that doesn't mean that we should accept what *can* be changed."

It was around this age that I learned that I loved to read, and from those books, discovered that I wanted

13

to be a teacher. In school, I realized that I was very smart, and that learning different subjects came very easy to me. The joy of learning was so overwhelming, that my favorite game to play with my siblings was "school". I would teach a concept, pass out papers, and assign tests with homework ready to be marked up with my red pen. My imitation of teaching came from a desire of being recognized for the wise student that I was in school.

All of my teachers were white, until I entered my sophomore year of college. Most of them were "superior" teachers, but some didn't seem to realize that they didn't treat their African American students with the same nurturing respect and encouragement that was extended to their white students. My intelligence was scrutinized with accusations of cheating that were all unsubstantiated. However, I was mostly met with indifference, only because I was shy. Like most children at this age, my sensitive, observant nature left me in a constant state of yearning for the verbal accolades that my peers and I deserved. As I advanced from grade to grade, I watched, with sadness, as many of my African American peers became detached from school and the desire for learning.

Dick and Jane books were the common readers assigned for instruction. While I loved those books, I was very aware that none of the characters were African American; none of them looked like me. The adventures of the children were so much fun, but I was always left feeling excluded from the experiences. I went to the library every chance I got. Every book I checked out was my temporary escape from home, and the bigotry surrounding me. Books about happy families, fantasy, mystery, saints, and crime solving dramas, were my favorites. I will never ever forget the feeling that I felt when my eighth-grade teacher assigned John Howard Griffin's *Black Like Me*. It was my first book about the African American experience, and is still one of my very favorite books to this day. I was captivated by Griffin, a journalist, who realized that he couldn't really know what it's like being a black person, unless he became black. I couldn't believe he shaved his head and engaged in treatments to turn his skin color to a convincing tone of black. Griffin was forever changed by the immense hardships African Americans faced, because of the color of their skin. I was saddened to learn he had succumbed to cancer from the carcinogenic effects of treatments he had endured to appear authentically African American.

When I was fifteen, three cars drove up to the curb in front of our house one day. My parents weren't home, and I had no idea why these cars were here at our house. The next thing I remember, is all ten of my siblings were being escorted to the cars by people identifying themselves as "social workers", and then being suddenly whisked away. The Department of Children and Family Services had been directed by a New York court to remove us from our home, and to charge my parents with child neglect. I remember some of my siblings crying as they were pulled away from the home. However, I distinctly remember an overwhelming sense of happiness as I got into one of the cars; I personally felt like I was being rescued from my toxic, dysfunctional home. After a short ride, three other younger siblings and I were placed in a foster care pre-placement shelter, while the seven younger siblings were placed in emergency foster care. I remember pleading to be placed in a loving foster home, but was told that they didn't place females girls of my age in foster homes. Since there was a shortage in group homes, I was conveniently tucked away in an all-female delinquency home. I was stunned to learn that my permanent residence would be with young women that were convicted of breaking the law, yet my only crime was being the child of African American parents, lacking the knowledge and skills to raise eleven children. I was angry, and decided that the rules for delinquent girls didn't apply to me. However, I quickly changed my mind when I learned my next home could be an all-female maximum security facility if I didn't learn to follow the rules. I decided the delinquency home was the lesser of two evils. I soon came to appreciate my safe environment, and the fact that my basic needs were met, but I was keenly aware that it lacked the loving and nurturing environment I longed for. While there in the facility, my mother visited once; my father also stopped in a couple of times. I soon accepted the fact that Wayside Home School for Girls would be my home base, until I graduated from Brockport State University.

The best decision I made while attending college, was to major in African American Studies as a sophomore transfer to Brockport State University in Brockport, New York. I remember during my tour of the college, and coming across a door with the sign African American Studies Department. It was fate that led me to open the door to inquire about the courses. It was then I decided to major in African American History and minor in Elementary Education. These courses changed my life in a profound way. As I learned the truth about the history and true survival of my people, amid unconscionable circumstances, I

16

gained a love and respect for myself, and of my people that I never thought possible. I had many awesome African American professors. Being in that atmosphere, I have a sense of personal pride knowing that several of them moved on to very prestigious careers; one even became the president of a college. My favorite African American professor was Dr. Herbert Douglas, who also became a lifelong mentor. Every one of my African American professors nurtured and encouraged their students. As a result of this experience, the love I had for myself became so intense, that I pledged I would include valuable African American history lessons daily as a teacher.

While writing children's books had always been an interest of mine, I found teaching, motherhood, and fifteen years of coaching, were full time jobs, sometimes leaving little time for anything else. It was only after I retired and started teaching on a part-time basis, that I started seriously thinking about writing.
One year, a student blurted out during class, "Why don't you write stories about all the lessons that you have been teaching us." Our class had been reading and discussing a newspaper article I had assigned about an African American issue. The student encouraged me by saying I should consider affecting other student's lives with my stories, the way I was affecting them. Soon, the rest of the class enthusiastically affirmed her statements by telling me specifically how much they appreciated me. Their feedback made me so emotional that I don't remember my response; I was too busy trying to hold back the tears. At the end of that school year, one of my students circulated a petition requesting that our administrators hire more teachers like me. I didn't seriously consider writing until the charter school where I was teaching, began to change management, and

17

ended up reassigning all of the teachers. It was then I made the decision to take a break from teaching for a while.

One day while reflecting and missing my days of teaching, I decided to sit down at the computer to begin writing my very first short story for *Wisdom Warriors*. I felt the title was quite fitting, since my father is from Sierra Leone, West Africa, where Africans believe in the wisdom of their elders. Based on these cultural traditions, I decided the grandparents, Grandpa Marv and Grandma Mary, would share valuable life lessons with their granddaughter, named Skye, throughout their daily interactions. The grandparents serve as an ideal model of immense cultural pride as Skye learns invaluable lessons to help her confront her daily challenges as a young African American person.

For years, people have discounted the systemic racism that pervades our public schools, and in the society in which we live in. The truth of the matter, is that too many African Americans, and other people of color, live amidst poverty, unemployment, unequal schools, poor housing, poor health care, and other dire hardships. Too many of our school teachers view diversity as a handicap, rather than an asset, often leaving African American students feeling unwanted and disengaged. Any student subjected to this kind of environment, and these daily hardships on a mass scale, is doomed to produce the same low school performance.

Eleanor Roosevelt said," No one can make you feel inferior without your consent." It is my goal through these stories, is to inspire love of self and culture, so that African American young people and other children of color refuse to grant permission, or to allow comments steeped in ignorance to cause them to feel inferior. I would also like for adults interacting with these young people, to also think of Maya Angelou's quote, "I've learned that people will forget what you said, people will forget what you did, but people will never forget how you made them feel."

I am living proof that students can thrive, despite dire hardships, when they are valued, nurtured, and given equal access to educational opportunities. Finally, I am hoping that all Americans, especially our young people of color, will read about the rich history of African Americans, because African American history, *is* American history.

Slave

Against my will

You blame me

You degrade me

You dehumanize me

You dehumanize yourself

Against my will

You blame future generations for their victimization

Leaving out the truth Tell the truth

Embrace your humanity

Honor me

Celebrate my contributions

Celebrate me

Mary Cole Watson, M. Ed.

Story 1

The best way to fight an alien and oppressive culture is to embrace your own.

African Proverb

Culture: The Beauty You See

Skye loves her grandparents. She always looks forward to Grandpa Marv picking her up after school. She always enjoyed spending time with him until her mom got off work. Grandpa Marv is fun. Grandpa Marv always makes Skye feel as if she's the most important person in his world when they're together. He tells Skye that her mom can make sure that she completes her homework at home, because this is his time with her to do what they want.

Skye's eyes lock onto Grandpa Marv, who is patiently waiting for her on the sidewalk as she pushed her way through the exit doors of the school hallway. With a big grin and the anticipation of the next few hours spent with him, Skye thinks to herself, "He's so funny." They lock hands and begin their chatter filled conversation for the next block and a half to the house.

Once inside, Grandpa Marv walks to the kitchen to grab their "secret snacks and drinks" to place on a tray as they settle in for the afternoon. Grandpa Marv says Grandma Mary and Skye's parents are too hung up on eating only healthy food. He tells Skye that their small amount of "secret treats" won't ruin their health, or their appetite before dinner.

As Grandpa Marv follows Skye to his favorite roomy space, his "man cave," Skye starts planning how she can avoid their normal conversation while watching television. She starts eating snacks. Skye usually sits next to Grandpa Marv as he searches for the channel, rearranging the snacks on the tray for easy access. Today, Grandpa Marv decided to watch a recording of his favorite women's basketball team. In the moments before the game comes on, Skye strategically positions herself on the floor beside Grandpa Marv. As she watches him search for the beginning of the game, Skye suddenly smiles as she remembers a funny story her mom told her about Grandpa Marv coaching her elementary school team. Grandpa Marv has always been a fan of basketball, but he especially began to enjoy women's basketball when Skye's mom once dreamed of playing in the WNBA. Skye couldn't help giggling when Grandpa started instructing the team on the television as if it were his first time watching the video. As Grandpa looked down at Skye laughing at him, he reached down and started rubbing Skye's head full of very thick curls.

He started laughing with her, and bent down to make nose to nose contact, as they always have in the past. Skye loved when Grandpa Marv ran his fingers through her hair and rubbed his nose against hers. But today, she doesn't think she ever wants him to do these things again. In fact, Skye doesn't even think she wants to be the same dark brown color as Grandpa Marv anymore.

Skye finds herself thinking about how she used to laugh with glee when Grandpa Marv rubbed her curls and made her nose tickle. Her face would light up with pride when Grandpa Marv would hold his arm next to hers to show her that they were exactly the same color. However, this time, Skye doesn't smile when Grandpa Marv takes hold of her arm to show their shared complexion. Realizing, something's wrong, Grandpa Marv wrinkles his forehead, and raises an eyebrow, and says, "Oh no, I've picked up the wrong kid from school today! We must rush back to school right away so I can get my granddaughter, Skye." Skye usually laughs at grandpa's corny jokes, but today she just looks at him as tears drop from her cheek and she moves to the sofa across the room. Grandpa Marv suddenly looks serious and says, "What's wrong, Skye?" in a very concerning tone.

As Skye tries to hold back her tears, she reflects on the day's events at school. Her memory flashes back on her and her friends playing glamour girls on the playground. While the girls were all different shades of brown, and some were white, Skye had the darkest shade of them all, and was the only one with thick black curly hair. One of the girls made the comment that they needed to "move out of the sun" so she wouldn't get "dark" like Skye. Her friend didn't know she had hurt Skye's feelings, and in doing so, made her feel inferior to her. Then another girl told Skye that if she really wanted to look glamorous, she should straighten her hair. Another one of the lighter skin toned black girls blurted out, "I'm going to get a straightened blond weave and a narrow nose job when I grow up!" Suddenly, Skye found herself wishing her skin were a lighter color, maybe even white. She found herself thinking she would be "glamorous" if her hair were straight, and not have any kinky curls.

"I don't want to talk about it Grandpa," she said as she folded her arms and turned away from him in shame. "Besides, you can't fix my problem. No one can." Recognizing that something was seriously bothering Skye, he got up from his chair and sat at the other end of the sofa. "Skye, you don't know that for sure now do you?" he said in a very soft, loving tone. He continued, "Grown people know things that young people don't because we have lived a long time, and have had lots of the very same problems. Grandpas can help fix lots of things for their grandchildren, if given the chance." Still ashamed to look at him, Skye said, "But I know you can't fix this problem that I have Grandpa." As Grandpa Marv inched a little closer to Skye, he touched her shoulder and said in the kindest voice Skye had ever heard, "Try me." Skye slowly unfolded her arms, and turned toward Grandpa, while wiping her tears. All the while, she was trying to decide how to tell Grandpa Marv what was on her mind, without making him feel sad as her friends made her feel.

"Grandpa, I don't like my curls anymore, and I wish my nose wasn't so wide," explained Skye. Bursting into tears again, Skye blurted out, "I don't want to be the same color as you anymore!" Wiping away more tears and trying to catch her breath, Skye slowly looks up at Grandpa Marv affectionately staring at her, but

24

not saying anything. He then holds Skye's chin in his hand, and looks at her with sad eyes and says, "It's time that we have a very special talk, because I know why you feel this way." Grandpa Marv picked Skye up and put her on his lap as she sobbed into his shirt. He waited for her to stop crying, and then he said, "I can fix your problem, but not in the way you think." Using the remote still in his hand, Grandpa Marv turned off the television. "Skye, I am going to tell you a story that you need to listen to very carefully." Skye nodded her head in agreement and listened very intently, because she knew Grandpa Marv was positioning himself as a *Wisdom Warrior*. This is what Skye decided to call Grandpa Marv and Grandma Mary when they said, "listen very carefully." When Skye's grandparents have these very serious talks with her, she sees them more as warriors - brave and experienced elders who help her understand things in her life today, based on events from the past. Grandpa Marv looks right into Skye's eyes and says, "You don't like your hair, your nose, and your skin color, all because someone made fun of all three. Right?" With amazement, Skye replies, "How did you know, grandpa?"

"Remember, I said that grownups know some things because they have lived a long time, and have had some of the same problems as you have? Well, I figured out a way to solve your problem," he said with a sense of pride. Grandpa Marv explained, "Skye, our ancestor's family, from long ago, lived in Africa, where it is so hot that their scalp would have burned, if it wasn't for the head full of thick coils of curls to protect it. Our beautiful hair is very different, and the textures of curls differ with each person, and in turn, the evolution of his or her people." As

25

Grandpa continued his explanation, he picked up one of Grandma Mary's magazines from the coffee table to display some of the latest styles showcased throughout the pages. As he fanned through the pages filled with beautiful brown people, he explained how the shape of African noses had to be wider, so to breathe easier in the harsh and intense heat. He told Skye that darker skin tones naturally protect the skin from being burned by the intense sun. The more Grandpa Marv explained, the more Skye understood that she is beautiful and uniquely made, but Skye didn't feel much better because she was certain her friends would still make fun of her. Realizing Skye was still worried, Grandpa Marv asks, "Remember how I told you that I could fix your problem, but not in the way that you think?" "Yes," Skye said, not convinced. Grandpa continued, "Well, first of all, your hair, nose, and skin color are not the problem. They are features that make you so very beautiful and different from everyone else. Thank goodness you can't change any of those things," he laughs. Then he adds, "However, my dear, we can change people's attitudes. I'm going to tell your mom to make sure she signs me up for speaker day at your school, so that I can tell everyone stories of our special beauty."

"Really, Grandpa?" exclaimed Skye. "Yes, really," said Grandpa Marv as he grabbed her and gave her a big hug. Skye loved Grandpa Marv's story. As she loosened her grip around his neck, Skye decided, "Grandpa, I don't want to change anything about me now." Smiling with a sparkle of joy, he says, "What a relief! I thought I picked up the wrong kid from school." Grandpa Marv and Skye returned to eating their "secret snacks", because they realized Grandma Mary would be coming home soon.

Story 2

> **The question is not whether we can afford to invest in every child; it is whether we can afford not to.**
> Marian Wright Edelman

Low School Performance: Above the Rim

Sipping on coffee at the kitchen table, Grandma Mary finds herself reading the community newspaper about how so few black students get into the best magnet public high school in her community. As she takes another sip of coffee and reads the article yet again, as if additional information will magically appear, she takes a deep breath of disbelief. She reads about her community's reality, and she can't believe that the article makes no mention of the systematic inadequacies when educating low income children of color. As an educator with more than 30 years in both elementary and high school, Grandma Mary has witnessed how these children are the most likely to be labeled as "at risk," as if something were wrong with them. She found in her classes, that most black students, and other students of color, were just as intelligent as any of the

27

other students. Based on both experience and research, Grandma Mary is convinced that it is society that is "at risk" for denying African American, and other students of color, an equal opportunity to education and various educational opportunities for both the student and their parents. She believes that if families don't have to experience some of the most preventable hardships that are not encountered by middle income and wealthy students, they would have a better opportunity to perform better in school. So many of the students from her community schools live in very poor neighborhoods. They often don't have enough nutritional food to eat, and in some of the worse cases, the student may not even have heat or even lights during the winter months. Grandma Mary thinks it doesn't make sense for the school system to expect students deprived of an equal education and basic life needs, to score the same on exams and projects as students of privilege.

Grandma Mary remembers having to enlighten some teachers who mistakenly thought children with these kinds of challenges just didn't care about school. She had to help them understand that some the student's hardships made it difficult for them to pay attention in class, or even do their homework after school. Grandma Mary and other teachers learned that students sometimes acted out not because they were "bad," but because they were looking for a way to express their anger at their living situations, and the lack of control of what was happening in their lives. Grandma Mary knows in her heart that most teachers care about their students, but many might not realize that a lot of the "bad" behavior and bad grades, have more to do with a child having a bad life, rather than their intelligence.

Grandma Mary realized her passion for this issue came from the fact that she grew up in a poor family. Each time she read an article like this, it reminded her that the main reason she did so well in school as a student, was because she loved learning more than anything else. Her school work and activities, often took her mind off of her troubles at home.

Suddenly, Grandma Mary hears the steps of little feet traveling down the living room hallway. It was Skye. "Good morning, Grandma Mary," she says, as if she hadn't a care in the world. Grandma Mary nods, "Good morning, my sweetness." Skye goes to a very good school only a couple of blocks from their home, but there are also several students bussed in from some of the surrounding areas. These children are from various cultures and backgrounds. Many are Black, Latino, and from other ethnic backgrounds. A large portion of this student population is eligible for free breakfast and lunch, which makes Grandma Mary wonder how many of these kids need free dinner, too. There's seldom a day that goes by that Skye doesn't share a story or two about kids from other classes on her playground wearing summer clothes during winter months, or about them wearing clothes that don't fit, with tears and holes all over. While other children tease and bully these students, Skye often makes an extra effort to befriend them, because Grandma Mary told her all about how she grew up poor as a child.

As Grandma Mary watches Skye struggle to pour milk over her cereal, her thoughts travel to a conversation she and Grandpa Marv had about five of Skye's male classmates. Nino, Tave, Alonzo, Jameel, and Jamel, having shown themselves to be very smart and capable, but each of them tends to welcome poor grades as validation of their "street cred" as future pro sport athletes. One day, Skye told Grandpa Marv about how the five boys made fun of another student named Jared, who wanted to be a judge when he grew up. Grandma Mary smiled and remembered how impressed she was with Grandpa Marv, when he got involved in the community setting. She remembers how he and Skye invited the boys over to the house. After playing basketball, they all ate some snacks, and Grandpa had a good heart to heart talk about the importance of education. During that talk, Grandpa Marv told them that America would always inspire them to focus more on sports than on their education, but that education was far more important than sports. As a retired school counselor, Grandpa Marv, understood the challenges of maintaining a certain image among school peers. The *Wisdom Warrior* wanted the boys to know that no matter what career path they chose, they would need, education to prepare them for life's journey, and make them great thinkers so they could make the best life decisions. Grandpa Marv had no intention of discouraging them from wanting to be pro players; he just wanted them to know that there were so many other ways to make "big" money in other sports careers – all of which required a college education. Grandpa Marv ended his talk with the boys by telling them that an injury could take them out of the pro game permanently, but an education would keep them in the game of life forever. To help keep the boys focused on both their game skills and education, Grandpa Marv had the boys over regularly to play basketball games with him and Skye in the backyard. When the weather was bad, Grandpa Marv would take them to the neighborhood recreation center, where one of his good friends made sure there was always a court and hoop available for them.

As Skye finished her breakfast, Grandma Mary realized it was her day to pick Skye up after school. Grandma Mary rushed down the living room hallway to coordinate afterschool plans with Grandpa Marv. While Skye grabbed her backpack and jacket, Grandma Mary rushed toward Skye's school. Grandma Mary let Skye know that Grandpa Marv would pick her up from school this afternoon. She explained to Skye that she had a meeting with the principal, Dr. Ivy. As one of the many activity community school volunteers, Grandma Mary was already donating money to a fund that anonymously paid for school supplies. However, this morning's article encouraged her to increase the amount of money she currently gave for the holiday dinners and winter clothing. She was adamant in her belief that the fewer worries children have about life's problems, the easier it is for them to concentrate on learning. Skye's school principal agreed to meet with Grandma Mary to discuss ways to raise more money, so they could help support the students that had greater hardships than the rest of the students, so Grandma Mary wanted to make sure she was well prepared for this afternoon's meeting.

Grandpa Marv was at the curb looking in the opposite direction, when Skye ran out of the school building. "Hi, Grandma Mary", she said laughing as she pulled on his jacket sleeve. "Very funny," said Grandpa. Then he reminded Skye that Grandma Mary had a meeting with the principal about an important matter. Before she could ask why, Grandpa Marv, quickly said, "No, it has nothing to do with you." "Phew! I thought I was in trouble," she said with relief. Locking hands as they strolled toward the house, Skye asked what they were having for a snack. Looking down at her with a partial frown, Grandpa said, "Well, your Grandma Mary found my secret stash of our snacks and has hidden them from me." With a big bellied laugh, Grandpa Marv explained that Grandma Mary confessed she had a feeling something was up because Skye never talked about the snacks she and Grandpa Marv ate when they got home. Grandma Mary said those suspicions were confirmed when Skye quickly changed the subject to avoid answering her inquiries about the snack of the day. "Oh no," said Skye. But Grandpa Marv reassured her she hadn't done anything wrong, and that Grandma Mary wasn't mad at all. "In fact, she thought it was funny," he added. With guilty chuckles Grandpa Marv said, "And imagine, she accused me of wanting to be your favorite grandparent."

"Oh, grandpa, that is so funny! I love both of you the same, and I actually like most of Grandma Mary's snacks anyway. It's just that your snacks are my favorite," said Skye as she raised her hand against her cheek. "I feel the same way," said Grandpa. As they entered the house, Grandpa Marv made his way to the kitchen, explaining that Grandma told him before he picked Skye up where the secret stash was hidden. "In fact, Skye, Grandma Mary told me that I don't have to hide them anymore. She agreed that you do eat mostly healthy food, so she doesn't mind what I give you since I give you small portions," he explained.

"Cool," said Skye.

"So how about a *cool* lemon Italian ice, young lady?" Grandpa Marv said with a big smile.

After Grandpa Marv and Skye finished their snack, Grandpa pulled out his chess set. "What is that grandpa?" asked Skye.

"It's called chess," he said. In his familiar **Wisdom Warrior** voice, Grandpa Marv explained that chess was a game that was played as early as 600 A.D, which was a long, long time ago. He explained that the game originated in Northern India, and like popular games today, it soon spread to Persia. It was noted for the patience, wisdom, and skill required to defeat one's opponent. Soon, the game gained more fame in the Muslim world after the Arab people conquered Persia. The game eventually evolved into a competitive sport. Once it reached the Southern European soil, it evolved. "Skye, you know I saw a story on the news yesterday about an eight-year old African homeless boy who won the chess championship for his age group. As I listened to his story, I believe he is the perfect example of doing incredible things despite tremendous hardships. People of all cultures from around the world were so impressed with his accomplishment, that they donated over one hundred thousand dollars for him and his parents to get an apartment. He became a champion after only one year of playing. Today, I am going to use his words to tell you why I am teaching you chess," explained Grandpa Marv. Staring at Skye eyeball to eyeball, Grandpa Marv said, "He told the reporter interviewing him that the game of chess is great practice for critical thinking and it's fun!" Grandpa went on to tell Skye that he thought chess would also add some challenge and variety to the game days with her school friends. This reminded Skye of the success story she forgot to share with him on their walk from school.

"Oh, Grandpa, I forgot to tell you that your talks with my friends are working. Nino, Tave, Alonzo, Jameel, and Jamel are paying more attention in class, and their grades are almost like mine. I knew they were smart, Grandpa, but it seemed as though they didn't want other people to know it. I think it wasn't just because they wanted to be pro athletes, I think it was because they didn't think people cared if they were smart or not."

"Skye, you impress me more and more every day with your ability to think deeply. You are going to ace this game, but you are not going to ever beat Grandpa," he responded in laughter.

"Oh yes, I will!" grinned Skye.

While Skye didn't beat Grandpa Marv this time, she developed an appreciation for the game, and picked up on its strategies quickly just as Grandpa Marv predicted she would. She liked the game so much that she told Grandpa Marv that she wanted to play chess the next time that he picked her up from school. "Okay," said Grandpa. "I will invite my friend Bernard who taught me to play the game to come over and see you play. He will be impressed." Grandpa Marv and Skye were having so much fun playing chess that they lost track of time. It was already time for Grandpa to take Skye home. He knew her mother and father would be anxiously awaiting her return. Grandpa Marv grabbed his hat, and Skye her jacket and backpack, and into the car they climbed. Before they knew it, Skye was already home. "Bye, Grandpa," she said as she gave Grandpa Marv an extra hug before getting out of his car.

Story 3 ███████████

The child who is not embraced by the village will burn it down to feel its warmth. African Proverb

Colorism: Baby, Oh My Beautiful Baby

Grandma Mary and Grandpa Marv were sitting at the kitchen table just as they had every Sunday morning since they first married. Their never changing routine included a fresh, squeezed glass of orange juice, a healthy breakfast with a half slice of toast shared between them, and both the local and national newspapers split between them both. Grandpa Marv favored the local paper, while Grandma Mary preferred the national paper. Their weekly practice has served a strategic purpose over the years. By reading different papers, Grandpa Marv and Grandma Mary shared interactive and engaging conversation with each other as they reviewed and discussed what the other had read. Grandma Mary reads the national news for important world views. Her favorite section of the national paper is the Book

Review section. She enjoys reading summaries of the most recommended books for people of all ages.

Grandpa's favorite section of the newspaper is the sports page.

Today the front page of Grandma Mary's Book Review was especially engaging. She found herself staring at a replica of a book cover displaying a beautiful, water colored picture of a very pretty dark skinned girl around Skye's age, looking at herself in a mirror. The reflection opposite the girl was a mirror image, except the image had white skin and white facial features. Grandma Mary spent several minutes just staring at the image. She remembered as a child, seeing herself in the same manner. Grandma Mary remembers wanting to be white, because she felt like whites were highly valued. Most black parents try to reassure their children that they are just as beautiful and valued as any other child. But, children of color find it difficult to be confident in their skin, without someone to model what that confidence looks like. Children of color are often barraged with images of success, intelligence, and pride through television and video games. Unfortunately, these images are filled with mostly white people. Just telling kids of color to feel good about themselves, is often a confusing message, when so many parents of color don't or can't show the children that they love what these images look like. As an educator who studied African American History, Grandma Mary learned about the horrible treatment of blacks passed down from slavery, and that the miseducation of an entire ethnic group has systematically diminished the self 'esteem and self-value from generation to generation.

Suddenly, Grandma Mary hears the rustle of little feet moving around upstairs. She realizes Skye is waking up from watching movies with her grandparents during her sleepover. Skye's mom and dad dropped her off late last night, so they could go to a concert together. As Grandma Mary returns her attention back to the newspaper book summary, she is reminded about the conversation Grandpa Marv recently told her he had with Skye, and how the value of her beautiful dark skin, wide nose, and kinky hair curls, were just as beautiful as anyone else's. Grandma Mary finds herself upset at the way America advertises to the world that it considers white culture most "desirable". She is concerned that America all too often, communicates to people of color that white beauty is more important than any other standard beauty. Even when models of color are on billboards or magazines, their complexion is mostly light skinned, lacking the distinctive features recognized in most people of color. Grandma Mary believes that if something is advertised to a young mind long enough, that young minds will begin to desire the product and the results it may claim, even if it's bad for them. Grandma Mary thinks to herself, "Beauty can be found in skin tones of all colors, all textures of hair, different body shapes, and unique, stunning facial features."

Grandma Mary hears Skye as she descends down the stairs. "Good morning Skye," they both said in unison. "We decided to let you sleep in this morning since we stayed up late last night," said Grandpa Marv. Skye went over to Grandma Mary to give her a kiss when she noticed the picture Grandma Mary was still examining. "Grandma Mary, why do the black girl and white girl look like the same person?"

37

"They are the same," said Grandma Mary. "Look closely." Skye raises her eyebrows as she remembers her talk with Grandpa Marv. "Oh, I get it. She sees herself as white when she looks in the mirror." "Yes, you're right," said Grandma Mary." As Skye makes her way across the room to give Grandpa Marv a kiss and hug, Grandma instructs her to get dressed because her parents were on their way to pick her up for breakfast.

Later that day, Grandma Mary enters the home of her good friend Jean, who was hosting a baby shower for her daughter Miranda. As she entered, she could feel the welcoming atmosphere filled with the fragrances of good food, good friends, and the anticipation of another generation. Grandma Mary made her way into the beautifully decorated home, that just happened to have been designed by Skye's mother, Madison. "Mary, so good to see you," says Carol, the guest of honor's mother. "Oh, Carol, it's so great to see you too," expressed Grandma Mary as they hugged.

Grandma Mary soon found the perfect seat facing the entryway. She enjoyed watching the guests enter the home and gush over her daughter's finished décor. The shower was open to women from throughout the community, each one just as beautiful as the next. Grandma Mary soon found herself thinking about this morning's article once again. As she watched the women interact with one another, she wondered how many of these women found comfort in their unique beauty. "There are women of African, Indian, European, Alaskan, and even Hawaiian descent represented in this very room," thought Grandma Mary. She pondered the fact that each individual had their own story of battling self-image, whether it was the color of their skin, the shape of their body, or the desired facial features shaped by deceptive images of "true beauty."

Grandma Mary was so lost in her thoughts that she didn't realize that many of the guests had already begun fixing their plates. "Mary, aren't you going to help yourself to some refreshments?" asked Carol, interrupting Grandma Mary's thoughts. "Oh, yes," said Grandma Mary as she rose from her chair to get in the short line, now forming at the dining table. "Mary, you were so deep in thought. What were you thinking about?" asked Carol as they were walking toward the dining room. "Oh, I was just thinking about a book review I read this morning about colorism." Admiring the diversity of Carol's many guests, Grandma shared her thoughts on how important it is for parents to promote positive self-imaging in their children.

Soon Grandma Mary, Carol and other guests were sharing some of their cultural experiences centered on skin tones. Linda, who was of European descent, described how she would spend hours in the sun for the perfect tan that she was sure would make her just as beautiful as her friends. Sofia, a native of Africa, shared how she would try to avoid the sun, in hopes her skin tone would lighten, helping her resemble more of the "American" definition of beauty. Each story, explaining the unrealistic goals of defined beauty, was just as detailed as the next. Throughout the conversation, Grandma Mary found herself resisting the desire to share the results of the 1940s "Clark Doll" experiment that conclusively demonstrated that "prejudice, discrimination, and segregation" created a feeling of inferiority among African-American children, which damaged their self-esteem. Furthermore, the experiment recently reenacted only to find very little has changed in almost eighty years later. When given the choice of dolls identical in every way, except color, participants gave positive responses to questions about the white doll and negative answers to questions about the black doll. Still, the majority of the girls wanted the white doll. Grandma Mary, and most people who know about the experiment, believe it proves that black children tend to feel devalued, even though no one culture is superior to another. Grandma Mary wants all children of color to feel that they matter just as much as any other child.

The conversation was cut short when Carol, the hostess, announced the games were about to begin. Ironically, the first game was to see who could diaper and dress their baby doll the fastest. The next game was to see who could come closest to the name of the baby when given only the first letter of its name. There were four more games and then the honoree, Miranda, opened up lots of very nice gifts. Grandma Mary smiled as she watched Miranda admire the many gifts, she received for her first baby, which was due next month. The rest of the shower was spent in conversation, and sure enough, Grandma Mary heard some ladies next to her discussing what they thought the baby might look like. The women shared some of the myths of how a mother can tell the possible complexions of their child by looking at the skin closest to the nail bed or the ears. As Grandma Mary listened, she wondered how much longer her people will have this conversation. She thought, "We as Americans need to see the beauty of all of the people who live in our country." Suddenly Grandma interjects, "As parents, we need to have a much different conversation about defining beauty, and how it is advertised, rather than promoting the use of dangerous bleaching creams and plastic surgery to change what is already beautiful." Suddenly, guilty expressions replaced the smiles of all of the guests in the room. Carol follows with, "I completely agree with you, Mary."

After helping Carol tidy up after most of the guests had left, Grandma Mary hugged her good friend and made her way to her car. While driving home and recalling the day's events, Grandma Mary had an idea. She loved a new television show where the host and guests sat at a round table, and honestly discussing difficult and important topics like those touched upon at the baby shower. The show's ultimate goal is to inform and inspire, exactly what Grandma Mary wants to do. She decided she would sign up for a room at the local library to have monthly discussions on subjects like the ones she had with Skye this morning, and the ladies at the baby shower. She concluded she would read the book on colorism mentioned in this morning's book review, to kick-off the first discussion topic.

Grandma Mary couldn't wait to tell Skye about her idea when she picked her up from school tomorrow.

Story 4

> **The great force of history comes from the fact that we carry it within us, are unconsciously controlled by it in many ways, and history is literally present in all that we do.**
>
> James Baldwin

African American History Month:
Our Moment to Shine

It's February, and it's cold outside. Skye and her friends look forward to the warmer weather so they can go outside to play on the playground. Until then, they have to stay inside where they would stay warm. Sometimes, during indoor recess, they are allowed to play games, color pictures, or make origami figures with construction paper. Skye was already trying to decide what her recess activity was going to be.

Ms. Graham began today's class by announcing that it was African American History Month, and to help celebrate, she introduced the Carter G. Woodson poster. As she read the paragraph below his picture, Skye noticed her teacher didn't really seem interested in his accomplishments and contributions to honor black Americans, since our traditional history books didn't. After reading the history filled paragraph, Ms.

Graham reminded the class to read the other posters hung on the wall when they took their five-minute daily breaks. As Skye studied the twenty posters neatly hung on the walls, she wondered why the teachers put the same posters up every year. Skye knew African American History Month was created to honor the contributions of black Americans, but didn't understand why they only displayed these few contributors each year. She thought even though all of the people on the posters were very famous, it made the students think they were the only people that contributed to African American history.

As the day continues with various activities, Skye's favorite activity has finally arrived, reading. Ms. Graham advises the class it is silent reading time when Skye's class has twenty minutes to read from their selected chapter books kept at their individual desks. Usually, Skye is excited when the teacher announces that it is time for silent reading. Skye often tells her friends that she doesn't know what falling in love with a person means, but she's sure she knows the feeling of falling in love with reading. While Skye's book is very interesting, she can't seem to concentrate on it. Instead, she observes the twenty posters hanging in the distance. Skye thinks to herself, "Because our teacher didn't make a big deal about African American History month, students won't be willing to give up their free time to read the accompanying informational paragraphs beneath their faces."

Suddenly, Skye notices Ms. Graham giving her a stern look. Her teacher noticed she wasn't really reading her book. Skye quickly looks down toward her book, but continues to read her thoughts instead of the words on the page. Before she realizes it, Skye's twenty minutes are over, and it's time for lunch, then recess. During recess, the children scrambled about the classroom, finding things to play with. Skye didn't really feel like talking or playing today since her best friend Marlene was absent. Other friends tried to get Skye to join them in their games, but she just sat on the cushioned chair under the construction paper Palm Tree, her and Marlene's "special inside spot" when they want to talk about "important matters." Skye found herself remembering a class presentation with a speaker named Bobbi Shumsky, a Jewish Holocaust survivor, who came last month. The speaker even had a film that the student's watched over two days that helped explain how the Nazis put her relatives in concentration camps, where they were killed by different forms of torture. Ms. Shumsky explained the definition of the Jewish Holocaust as the destruction, or slaughter on a mass scale, of the Jewish population. Skye considered the history her grandparents shared with her about how masses of slaves were destroyed or slaughtered. She didn't understand why her teachers didn't talk about the "African Slave Holocaust." Skye's thoughts were interrupted by the bell ending recess.

It was much easier for Skye to concentrate for the rest of the afternoon since she had her two favorite specials of art and music. When school was over, Skye met Grandma Mary in the car rider's line, where she picked her up.

"Hi, Grandma Mary," Skye said as she kissed her and buckled her seatbelt. "Hi Love," Grandma Mary said, as they followed the other cars out of the school driveway.

44

Skye enjoyed her and Grandma's review of the day on the short drive home.

"What did you do in school today?" asked Grandma Mary. Grandma Mary strategically asks Skye what she did in school, rather than how school was, as she did in the past. When asked "how was school today," Skye would mostly reply with, "nothing special." Now, when Grandma Mary asks, "What did you do?", she gets more details and can easily tell how Skye's day has been by her detailed answer. Skye began telling Grandma Mary all about how Ms. Graham introduced African American History Month, and how the students are supposed to read the poster paragraphs during their class breaks for the month. Then Skye asked, "Grandma Mary, I know why we have African American History month. But how come people don't really treat it as special as they treat the Holocaust? Every school year we have speakers and films for the Jewish Holocaust, but not for African American History. At least Ms. Drake, my third-grade teacher, had our class do reports on historically recognized African Americans. Grandma, I know I'm supposed to be happy when February comes, but it makes me sad. Some of the kids ask why African Americans should have a special month, when there's not one for white Americans. I'm surprised that they don't realize that we study their history every day in school." Surprised and elated with how much thought Skye had put into today's events, Grandma replied, "Well, I'm really glad that I am going to teach you how to knit today. You've asked some great questions, and I can feel how sad you are today." Grandma continues, "I planned to teach you to knit a scarf for yourself to use next winter. Moving your fingers in the way that you do to knit helps relax a person as they create something beautiful." Feeling excited at the new experience, Skye asks, "Is knitting hard, Grandma Mary?" Grandma Mary replies, "Not the knitting I'm going to show you. But yes, some things are complicated to knit."

After arriving at the house and pulling into the garage, Skye and Grandma Mary walk into the house where Grandma Mary already has some plain yogurt, bananas, and blackberries mixed in a bowl. "Oh, cool," said Skye. "This is my very favorite healthy snack." Grandma Mary smiles as she holds Skye's chin in her hand, "I must have known you would need something to cheer you up."

Realizing it was a little too chilly to sit outside, yet also a beautiful day to enjoy the sunshine, Grandma Mary moved her and Skye's project to the sunroom, just off the patio. Skye loved the patio area. She would turn on Grandma Mary's water fountain and sit on the lounge chair to read her books on nice days. After settling into her favorite chair, Grandma Mary took out a huge bag filled with knitting needles and lots of different colored yarn. Skye picked the purple yarn and thick needles because Grandma Mary said the thicker needles made a loose pattern instead of a tighter one like the smaller needle.

Grandma Mary began showing Skye knitting pattern examples of tight, loose, large, and small projects from her bag. Then she asked Skye how wide she wanted her scarf to be before showing her how to "cast on," the first step of attaching the yarn to the needle. As she and Skye began their project, Grandma Mary went into her *Wisdom Warrior* mode, and explained the history of knitting to Skye. Grandma Mary explained that while the exact origin and history of knitting is not clear, research suggests the oldest known knitted object was an 11th Century pair of socks found in Egypt on the continent of Africa. Grandma Mary stated that research also suggested that knitting evolved and then later spread to Europe via the trade routes.

After getting the hang of it, Skye knitted a few rows. Grandma Mary smiled with pride as she saw how fast Skye was catching on to knitting. Grandma Mary then placed her hand on top of Skye's as she told Skye to rest her knitting project on her lap. Grandma decided this was a good time to answer some of the questions Skye had in the car on the way home. Grandma Mary stood up to plug her cascading fountain in, because she knew it would make Skye feel calm and peaceful as she shared some very difficult facts with her.

Grandma Mary explained to Skye that knitting and goods weren't the only things traded on the routes from Africa. She explained to Skye that historians estimated that between 12,000,000 and 14,000,000 Africans were captured, and even stolen from their families, to be sold into slavery. She went on to explain that millions of these Africans died due to horrible conditions from the Middle Boat Passage, between Africa and death raids once in America. In comparison, Grandma shared that most historians estimated approximately 5,000,000 to 6,000,000 Jews were killed in the Holocaust. So, by definition the Holocaust Ms. Shumsky talked about, could also be used to describe what happened to slaves throughout slave trade. Some people in our country do refer to the slave experience as the "African Holocaust", but that description has not been adopted as a general term in America.

"Skye, people don't know what they don't know," said Grandma Mary. She continued, "In other words Skye, an honest conversation about slavery hasn't taken place at your school, and unfortunately, slavery is not discussed, in depth, in our American History textbooks. One of Grandma Mary's sayings is, *"If a person is not part of the solution then they are part of the problem."* So educated blacks and every other ethnicity, must fight for their stories to be honored and discussed. All cultures deserve the same respect as members of *one* human race. African Americans deserve the upmost respect for the unspeakable treatment suffered during slavery, and because of the mass contributions we have made to this country, just as other ethnic groups do. African American History *is* American History!"

Taking heed to her own advice, Grandma Mary told Skye she would set up a meeting with her principal to talk about Skye's concerns and suggestions on how the community can join the effort to educate students about Black History, and ways to make African American History month more prominent in school. Grandma Mary said she would even ask to have a special speaker in recognition of the month of February. Then Grandma Mary looked at Skye and asked, "Now, what can you do to help with the problem?" Surprised at Grandma Mary's question, Skye replied, "I don't know Grandma Mary?" "You have already done something, Love." "You figured out that your school had a problem with celebrating African American History month, and recognized that both Jewish and African people suffered a holocaust."

"Grandma, that's because you taught me to always be concerned enough to ask questions until I'm old enough to make bigger decisions, and take action for myself," Skye grinned.

Glad to see that she was able to help Skye feel better, Grandma asked Skye, if she wanted to take her knitting home to work on. After careful thought, Skye replied, "I want to take it home." As they packed everything back into Grandma's bag, she said, "Okay, promise Grandma Mary that you won't work on it until all of your homework is completed."

"Promise," said Skye.

Story 5

You write in order to change the world... if you alter, even by a millimeter, the way people look at reality, then you can change it.

James Baldwin

Hip Hop: The Beat of a Different Drum

It was another perfect spring day. Grandpa Marv was leaving to pick Skye up from school, when he saw a huge beat up white van drive up to his next-door neighbor's house. The truck had black painted letters saying *Stanley Siding and Much More*. Before pulling out of the driveway, Grandpa Marv watched as four guys climbed out of the truck. Three of them, one black and the other two white, appeared to be younger workers, and the fourth, an older black man, who seemed to be in charge. He was pointing at the house, while instructing the other men how to begin the apparent project. As they all began pulling the deep blue siding and other materials out of the back of the van for Mr. Johnson's home, Grandpa Marv assumed they were all good friends by the way they smiled, laughed, and joked with one another, as they were setting up. Grandpa Marv's quiet street was busier than usual these last two weeks because it has been a detour route due to some construction work on a nearby street. It took five minutes before Grandpa Marv could back out into the street.

As Grandpa Marv pulled up to the curb, where Skye was already waiting, he noticed her smile seemed just a bit brighter than usual. "How's my girl?" Said Grandpa Marv as Skye hopped in and hugged his neck.

"Great!" Skye said. Surprised with her enthusiasm, Grandpa Marv responded, "And what makes it so great?" Skye explained that she really liked a new student in her class. Skye went on to describe the cultural dynamics of her class, and how most of the white girls didn't want to be with her and her black friends. Skye explained that Melissa, her new friend, wasn't like the other girls. Instead, she took turns and played with both groups. Surprised at such obvious segregation between the groups, Grandpa Marv asked, "Skye, what makes you think they don't want to be friends with you and your friends?" Skye very matter-of-factly explains, "The white girls look at us like there is something wrong with us. Once, I saw one of the girl's snicker and point at Nakia's newly braided hair. The girls with long hair are always flipping their hair when they go by us, as if their hair is more special than ours." Unaware of such demeaning happenings, Grandpa Marv responded in a questioning tone, "Hmmm. I see." Then he said, "So what makes your new friend so special?" "Well," began Skye, "after playing jump rope with the other girls, Melissa came up to us during recess and asked us if she could play with us. We were jumping double dutch when she came up to us. We were all a little surprised, but told her, yes. Grandpa, we were shocked that she could double dutch just as well as us, and she could turn the two ropes like she had been doing it for a long time. Melissa just acts natural around us. And she didn't ask us if she could touch our hair, or ask us why our skin was brown or tan. She treated all of us as is if we are no different than she. We could just be ourselves around her." "That is great," said Grandpa. Skye continued, "Grandpa Marv I think she may have moved from a neighborhood where there were black kids."

"I think that is a good guess," he said.

Going into his *Wisdom Warrior* mode, Grandpa Marv said, "Hopefully, Melissa will grow into adulthood with the same compassionate attitude. Unfortunately, so many times kids who are friends in childhood, don't remain friends because their parents fear their children will be exposed to the stereotypical characteristics by living, and growing up, around black children and families. In fact, some move out of the neighborhood when they think it is getting "too black", or they decide to accept society's unfounded definition of African Americans as they get older. When Grandma Mary and I moved into our neighborhood, it was occupied by predominantly white families. When your mother was three, an unwelcoming neighbor put a long nasty letter in our mailbox, telling us and the other families of color that we were not welcomed. We and most of the other families stayed, but we never joined the homeowner's association because they failed to stand up for us. No one in the association was brave enough to speak out against what that woman did. There was no way to know if she wasn't speaking for all of the other white families. "Wow, grandpa," said Skye in a soft surprised voice.

Grandpa Marv pulled into the driveway of the house, and Skye jumped out to run upstairs to change out of her school clothes. Grandpa Marv came in, hung his baseball cap, and began popping popcorn to go, also pouring the lemonade for him and Skye's after school snack. As Skye whisked down the stairs and sat at the kitchen table, she yelled, "Wow, Grandpa, I know what we are going to do today!" Grandpa Marv grinned as he sat the bowl of popcorn in front of them, "I knew you would see what it was from where you're sitting." Grandma Mary had redecorated and moved the table of plants from in front of the French doors, and now Skye had a clear view of the badminton on the grass in the backyard. Taking only a few kernels of popcorn, Skye jumped up and opened the doors onto the patio, skipping to the backyard. She excitedly opened the brand-new badminton set. After coaxing Grandpa Marv to skip the snack and to put the game in place, they were soon smacking the birdie back and forth over the net. A few minutes into the game, Grandpa Marv and Skye heard loud rap music coming from Mr. Johnson's backyard. It was the workers Grandpa saw earlier taking a break. Skye listened to the men having fun on their break: singing along to the lyrics of a song, laughing and joking. As the songs played, Skye heard the N word many times, then the B word, as well as the H word. Skye couldn't see the men, but she thought she had an idea of what they looked like, based on the thug and gangster song lyrics. Grandpa Marv looked disgusted! His first thought was to end the badminton game, go inside and close all the windows and put the air on, but he knew Skye would be crushed to end their game so

53

soon. While disturbed by the raunchy words, Grandpa Marv also knew that Skye had heard most of these songs as cars drove down the streets in the summer; not to mention that some of her school friends listened to and sang some of the same lyrics. Grandpa Marv decided to keep playing the game with Skye since he figured the workers break would be over soon. As he glanced over, he could see the workers were doing a pretty good job, at a fairly steady pace.

Sure enough, the music stopped next door after fifteen minutes, and after another 30 minutes of hitting the birdie back and forth over the badminton net, Grandpa Marv and Skye went inside. Skye was almost certain Grandpa Marv would talk to her about the music. She knew he was mad about the bad words, but she didn't know how to tell him she really likes the rap songs. Minus the bad words, Skye enjoyed the beat and rhythm. Instead of waiting for Grandpa Marv, Skye decided to start the conversation that she knew the *Wisdom Warrior* had prepared for her.

"Grandpa Marv, I know you're mad about the bad words in the songs those guys were playing," Skye said.

"Yes, Skye, you're right. But I am extremely disappointed about so much more than the words. It's the meaning of the words and what it says about miseducating youth like you. Don't get me wrong Skye, your Grandma Mary and I love rap. There are so many super talented rap artists out there that have very cool beats, fabulous voices, and perfect rhyme. But wrong is wrong. When your Grandma Mary and I were in college, we majored in African American

History. I remember in one of our classes, we read the books of Dr. Frances Cress Welsing, an American Afrocentrism psychiatrist, who offered a theory called "The Cress Theory of Color-Confrontation and Racism", also referred to as White Supremacy. She said that the African American culture is the only culture on Earth to use bad words to sing and praise ourselves. Welsing said that "if you teach people to think they are the negative words they call themselves, then they treat each other disrespectfully and believe that they are the meaning of the words." Cress Wesling also said, that "if the people themselves believe those words, they will always be taken advantage of by prejudice; people in power, who tend to agree with the descriptions they use to describe themselves." Grandpa looked into Skye's eyes and he said, "The worse outcome is that if we think so little of ourselves then we don't value our lives or the lives of our people."

As Grandpa Marv continued talking to Skye, he said that listening to those songs in the backyard, made him remember something Booker T. Washington said, "Evil doesn't become good just because it is accepted by the majority." Grandpa Marv went on to tell Skye that the B and H words, are among the most disrespectful words any man can call a woman; that these words simply encourage others to treat black women as less than a human being. The N word, as well as other thug and gangster words, used mainly to describe men, also could describe women, only encouraging people to become the meaning of those words. He explained that far too many rappers fail to really think about the meaning of the words they use in their songs, because singing those words tend to make them feel so powerful. Grandpa Marv expressed to Skye that he believes these rappers don't realize that they are agreeing with the former slave masters from long ago; that African Americans are all of those terrible words. He made clear that these rappers are being paid millions and millions of dollars, to have millions and millions of their fans think negatively about themselves. He explained that Grandma Mary and Grandpa Marv are convinced that rappers would be just as popular if they focused on positive words that uplift our people.

As Skye listened to Grandpa Marv, she realized that she should be more selective in the songs she listens to with her friends. She wanted to support rappers who made her feel good about herself and the people in her community. Skye concluded that it is every culture's tradition, and obligation, to respect their culture. She thought, our people, all people, need to remember that all cultures are supposed to pay honor to their ancestors. She also thought to herself, rappers who use bad words, that put our culture down are *not* honoring their ancestors, or themselves.

She looked at Grandpa with resolve, and said, "I understand Grandpa," As they hugged, Grandpa stood up, grabbed his hat and told Skye, "Time to go home, Brown Sugar." As they walked out of the house, Grandpa Marv locking the front door, and then getting in his car, and driving away.

Story 6 ████████

> *You may not control all the events that happen to you, but you can decide not to be reduced by them.* Maya Angelou

Stereotyping: Don't Pigeonhole Me

As Grandma Mary sits on the patio, enjoying the nature that surrounded her, she finds herself thinking about the changes taking place at Skye's school. Even though the Whitney Magnet Public School remains among the best in Brooklyn, New York, there have been a lot of changes over the last couple of years. Grandma Mary has noticed that several of the white parents have started moving out of the district, and some of the remaining black parents have expressed raising concern with the potential of lower educational expectations, as a result of black to white student ratio. As Grandma Mary sips on her tea, as she thinks about how unfortunate it is that several of these parents feel this way, solely because they choose to believe the negative stereotypes.

These parents believe simplified judgments without realizing there are individual differences in the groups of people whom they don't even know. Grandma Mary and Madison, Skye's mom, are planning to attend the first parent meet and greet with Dr. Ivy, Whitney Magnet Public's first black principal, that evening. Grandma Mary hopes that he will help the parents focus on their children's education, and not the unfounded stereotypes that are driving families out of the neighborhood, and in doing so, away from the school. According to the area newspaper and school website, Dr. Ivy graduated from Harvard University, and is an expert in elementary education, with ten years of experience as a principal. The article discusses how the new principal benefited from "affirmative action" as a star basketball athlete on scholarship. Many parents were surprised to learn that Dr. Ivy was extremely gifted in both education and basketball. The article also explained how Dr. Ivy came from a very poor family, like some of the students attending Whitney Magnet Public. It discussed how his family believed in being the very best one could be; at whatever they did.

Grandma hopes that tonight's meeting with Dr. Ivy will help dispel some of the stereotypes; to help parents to rethink their idea of moving away based on factual information, and not the unsubstantiated ideas of potential crime, poor education, and drugs in the area. Grandma Mary reflects on the fact that statistics show over 80% of the negative information presented by the media is presented from only one perspective, who were usually not people of color. Statistics show that because there are very few black or nonwhite writers promoted in front of, or even behind the camera, reports more often portray minorities negatively, and positive image suggestions are often rejected. Grandma Mary also believes that people generally think that a white principal is good for all students, but that the rest might not feel that a black principal is good enough for all students.

Later that evening, as Grandma and Madison entered the school auditorium, there was only enough room to stand. Without introduction, Dr. Ivy came to the stage, welcoming the parents who attended, and began sharing details about himself. He talked about his qualifications for the position, and his love of children and education. He expressed how important it is for *all* children to see a black person as principal, particularly African American children, because children often desire to be what they see before them every day. Dr. Ivy earnestly discussed his experience growing up in extreme poverty, to stress the point that poor children are just as capable of excelling in school when given equal educational opportunities, like those available at Whitney. He reiterated his commitment to the parents and their children, stating how he looked forward to working with the dedicated teachers and staff members at Whitney. He ended his talk by saying, "True inclusion of our different cultures is a strength that takes constant communication and understanding of untrue negative stereotypes." He pointed out as well that it is his hope to create a school environment where all children feel that they matter. For such a powerful speech, Dr. Ivy received a standing ovation.

It was already 9:00 P.M. when Madison dropped Grandma Mary off at her house. She could hardly wait to tell Grandpa Marv about the school meeting. She told Grandpa Marv that Dr. Ivy was everything a parent could ask for in a principal. She also told him about the standing ovation from all the parents that came to the meet and greet. Skye had been telling Grandpa Marv stories every day about something that Dr. Ivy said or did. She even told him that more black and white students were playing together on the playground and sitting together in the cafeteria. Skye said there was so much school spirit, that it felt like a family away from home. Grandpa Marv knew Skye doesn't exaggerate, but he was curious to hear what adults thought about Dr. Ivy. Now, Grandpa Marv was really looking forward to picking Skye up after school tomorrow to hear more about Dr. Ivy, and sharing with her all of what Grandma Mary thought of Dr. Ivy, too. Grandpa Marv was sure their discussion would be something new to talk about, since Skye's mother hadn't had a chance to tell her about the meeting, since she was in bed by the time her mother arrived home.

The next day, Grandpa Marv waited at the curb for Skye to get out of school. Skye was usually waiting with the other car riders when he pulled up. However, not today. Initially, Grandpa Marv didn't worry because the teachers were very watchful of the children, but he had started wondering what was keeping her. Just when Grandpa Marv was getting ready to go see what was keeping Skye, she came running out of the school.

"Sorry, I'm late, Grandpa," said Skye as she reached over to kiss Grandpa Marv's cheek. "Dr. Ivy called me to his office after school. Melissa was in his office too. Her mother can't pick her up today because she is stuck in traffic. There was a very bad accident on the highway. Melissa asked her mom if she could come home with me. Her mom told Dr. Ivy it would be okay, if you or Grandma Mary approved," explained Skye. "So, is it okay, Grandpa?" she asked. "Sure," Grandpa Marv said with a smile. "I knew you would say yes Grandpa!" Skye exclaimed as she opened the door to go back inside the school. Just as Skye was racing up to the door, Dr. Ivy and Melissa walked out. Grandpa Marv got out to greet Dr. Ivy, and told Dr. Ivy that he didn't mind taking Melissa home with him and Skye. With that, Dr. Ivy gave Grandpa Marv a number to call Melissa's mom for more information.

Skye and Melissa jumped into the backseat together. "Buckle your seatbelts," Grandpa said, as he buckled his. The two girls had already become good friends on the playground, so Skye was looking forward to Melissa coming over to her house. Grandpa Marv introduced himself as Mr. Hall, Skye's grandfather. Melissa leaned forward and said, "Hi, Mr. Hall. Thank you for letting me visit your house to play with Skye while waiting for my mom."

"It is a pleasure to have you visit," he responded." With excitement, Melissa then turned to Skye, "So, what are we going to do when we get to your house?" asked Melissa. Skye started telling Melissa about the snacks she often has with Grandpa Marv. As Skye told Melissa about Grandma Mary finding his secret snack stash, Melissa looked at the rearview mirror at Grandpa Marv and giggled. "What's for our snack today, Grandpa Marv?" asked Skye, who was also looking into the mirror. As he glanced at their smiling faces looking at him through the rearview mirror, he responded, "Chocolate chip cookies and almond milk." With a huge smile and raised eyebrows, Skye and Melissa yelled, ``Cool" in unison.

"When we are done eating our snack, I want to go outside to play hopscotch," said Skye. "What is that?" asked Melissa. Skye explained how Grandma Mary taught her how to play a few days ago. "I loved it," added Skye "Ok," grinned Melissa. Grandpa Marv enjoyed listening to the girls' lively conversation in the back seat of the car, and now in the kitchen while they ate their snack. "Let's go outside," Skye said. She found the colored chalk and started to draw some of the squares. She let Melissa draw some of the squares too. There were two squares then one square in the center above the two squares. The pattern was repeated until there were eight squares. Skye told Melissa to get a short stick and showed her how to play. "I love this game!" Melissa said as she hopped through the squares. Skye won, but Melissa almost beat her. The girls played two more times and split the wins between themselves. Just as they finished their last game, Melissa saw her mom drive up into the driveway. She parked her car on the side of the driveway and climbed out. She had long blond hair tied in a big top knot. To complement her hairstyle, she wore a black pantsuit, with a white shirt, and black pumps. Skye thought she looked just like Melissa. Grandpa Marv greeted her at the door and invited her into the house, with the girls following. He asked Skye to take Melissa up to her room to play while he had a moment to visit with her mom. The girls ran upstairs, while Melissa's mom introduced herself as Donna Spencer. She and Grandpa Marv talked about how both girls loved the new principal and the changes he has made. They also discussed the girls blossoming friendship. Donna told Grandpa

Marv that Melissa talked about Skye almost every day. She welcomed the opportunity to meet him due to the inconvenience of being stuck in traffic. Grandpa Marv shared, "I understand, and you should know that Skye feels the same way about Melissa."

Twenty minutes later, Donna was thanking Grandpa Marv as she called for Melissa to come down so they could leave. "Again, thank you so very much," said Donna as she started out the door. "Mom, I had such a great time!" exclaimed Melissa. "You can tell me all about it on the way home," said her mom. As Melissa and her mom started down the walkway, Skye yelled, "Ms. Spencer, can Melissa come over to play even when you're not stuck in traffic?"

"If your grandfather agrees, I would love that," said Ms. Spencer. "Fine by me," said Grandpa Marv as he hugged Skye and waved farewell to Donna and Melissa. As Ms. Spencer stepped into the car, she yelled back to Skye, "And I would love for you to come visit our home sometime too!" Both girls beamed with excitement. Preparing to close the passenger door, Melissa said, "Skye, I love being your friend." To which Skye replied, "You're pretty cool, too." Melissa waved from the window as her mom drove away.

"Well, Grandpa, do you like Melissa?" asked Skye. "Yes, Skye, I really like her personality, and the way you two played and communicated with each other., I am looking forward to her coming over to visit you again." Skye told Grandpa Marv that her other friend Marlene, likes Melissa too. Grandpa Marv smiled as he braced himself for Skye's next question. "Grandpa Marv, can Marlene come over when Melissa's here?"

"Yes, and I knew you were going to ask me that," smiled Grandpa Marv. "Now go get your things. It's time to take you home." As Skye skipped toward her backpack, she said "Thanks for letting Melissa come over, Grandpa Marv."

"You're welcome," he said, as they walked out of the house toward the car.

Story 7 ████████

> *Wrong is wrong, no matter who does it or says it.*
> Malcolm X

Bad Words: Words Matter

Today, Skye finds herself daydreaming about the fun awaiting her. Her mind is filled with excitement because Grandma Mary is going to pick her up from school today so they can go plant a vegetable garden. Skye loves school, but she is so excited that she can't concentrate on the science lesson her teacher, Ms. Drake, was teaching. Suddenly, all the students are looking her way. "Why are they looking at me," she thought.

"Skye, I'm waiting for a response to my question," said Ms. Drake. Skye was embarrassed because she didn't hear the question, and therefore couldn't answer the question. "Uh, I don't know," stammered Skye. "Really, you don't know what the weather is like outside? You're sitting by the window!" Everyone started to giggle and Skye wished that she could disappear as she did in her daydream.

Luckily, Ms. Drake didn't want to embarrass her any more than she had, so she asked Skye's friend Marlene the same question. Skye knew Ms. Drake was going to talk to her later about her daydreaming, so she made sure that she was ready to answer any other questions that Ms. Drake might asked her. But Ms. Drake didn't ask her any more questions. Soon, it was almost time for recess and Skye was concerned Ms. Drake might hold her back to talk about her not paying attention. Skye loved recess because she loved sports, the gossip, and spending time with her friends; just having fun.

"Recess," Ms. Drake announced, and then came the dreaded, "Skye, may I see you for a moment?" Skye went up to Ms. Drake's desk, but to her surprise Ms. Drake told her to enjoy recess and that she wanted to have a word with her after school. "Can we talk now, Ms. Drake?" Skye uttered as tears streamed down her face. Surprised at Skye's response and tears, Ms. Drake said, "I thought you loved recess?" "I do, but Grandma Mary is picking me up right after school and we are going to plant a garden of my very favorite vegetables," explained Skye. "Well, I now know why you weren't paying attention," said Ms. Drake, with a slight smile. "Since you usually pay attention in class, there will be no consequence today," conceded Skye's teacher. Feeling relieved, Skye smiled and thanked Ms. Drake, as a recess monitor, walked her outside to the jungle gym.

Instead of playing today, Skye decided to sit on the bench under the giant oak tree to talk to her friend Marlene. Skye wanted to tell Marlene all about her plans to plant vegetables with Grandma Mary later this afternoon. Just as they sat down, both girls saw two boys push each other and call each other a very bad name beginning with the letter N. There were no adults around to see or hear what the boys were saying, and then they went back to chasing each other on the playground. A few minutes later, Skye heard the word again. This time, two girls were just talking like Skye and Marlene. All the children were used to hearing bad words on the playground, but this was the first time Skye heard this very bad word on the playground, and no adults close by hearing what was said. Skye was confused about how and why the word was bad, because the two black girls were just using it like it was an ordinary word, and the white boys used it as an insult toward the black boy while shoving each other. Skye decided she would ask Grandma Mary, her *Wisdom Warrior*, later. Skye loved the fact she could ask Grandma Mary or Grandpa Marv, about anything and on any subject. They always explained their answers in a way that she completely understood.

Before Skye knew it, recess was over and they were back in class. Ms. Drake asked Skye a question from the history lesson, and this time, Skye answered the question as Ms. Drake winked at her. As soon as school was over, Skye rushed out to meet Grandma Mary. Grandma Mary greeted her with a huge hug and kiss before Skye got in her SUV. Skye decided to ask Grandma Mary her question now, because she didn't want to talk about bad things while she was planting the vegetables in the garden. "Grandma Mary, why do people use the N word when they are not mad, or even when they are?" Before Grandma Mary could answer, Skye continued, "The two black girls were just using it while talking to each other, and then two boys said the word when they were mad at

67

each other." Grandma Mary could see that this was a very concerning matter to Skye. So, she said, "Why don't we just talk about your school day on the drive home and I will answer your question while we eat our snack before we go out to plant." Skye wondered what the healthy snack would be. Her body loved healthy snacks, but she also liked when she and Grandpa Marv would eat her favorite candy snacks.

Grandma Mary pulled out the hummus and rice cakes with lemon water when they arrived at the house. When they sat on the porch., Grandma Mary began to explain the word. "Skye," she calmly said, "Unfortunately, that word is very popular. Just because something is popular, doesn't mean it is right." She told Skye that the word is the worst insult one could call someone. Grandma Mary explained that it was first used hundreds of years ago by some very bad white people, who did some very, very bad things to black people. Grandma Mary said the word will always have a bad meaning, as it was used by the two boys. Looking at Skye with sadness, Grandma Mary then told Skye that many black people today decided they would try to turn the bad meaning around to make it more of an ordinary word, even as a greeting, or even in regular conversation. Then Grandma Mary explained that some black people tried to justify the word used by certain white people, considering them as friends, so they in turn could use the word, but that didn't include other white people; because some used the word in very bad situations.

Skye finished her snack, but Grandma Mary hadn't touched hers. This was the first conversation Skye and Grandma Mary had during their snack where

Grandma Mary didn't eat. Deeply concerned with the depth of this conversation, the **Wisdom Warrior** said, "Skye, you must think for yourself and ask yourself important questions before making important decisions." Grandma Mary pulled out a dictionary and read the definition out loud of the *N* word, "a very bad term for a black or dark-skinned person." Grandma Mary then asked Skye to ask herself, if she considers the N word a bad word, or a word to use in conversation?

"I think it's a bad word," Skye replied. Grandma then asked Skye to consider if prejudice people thought the slight change in spelling, intended a positive definition, that changed their perception of the word. Still contemplating the question, Skye asks, "Is that definition in the dictionary?"

"No," replied Grandma Mary. Skye then definitively answered, "Then I think they believe the bad definition. I also think white people don't care what we do to the word to change it, because they know most people will believe the dictionary meaning." Then Grandma asked, "Do you think your African ancestors would want anyone to use that word?"

"No," Skye said, shaking her head. "And do you think you should honor your ancestors by doing what they would want, instead of what is popular?" Grandma Mary continued. Nodding in affirmation, Skye replied "Yes, I should do what my ancestors want."

"Your answers make perfect sense," said Grandma Mary. "It is my hope that one day our people will realize that any positive meaning they give the word, is not more important to the meaning that the word, in all its forms, would mean to our ancestors. Sometimes we have to sacrifice our own selfish needs for the sake of people who have suffered, so that we could be free," explained Grandma Mary. "I get it, Grandma Mary," said Skye.

"Now let's go out to plant," said Grandma Mary, as they put on their floppy hats and raced out to the soil.

Story 8

The service you do for others is the rent you pay for your room here on earth.

Muhammad Ali

Poverty: A Present with a Past

Grandma Mary knew this day would come. Skye is so very bright and asks questions all of the time. Grandma Mary loves that Skye is curious, because she knows the more curious a person is, the more they learn; the more they learn, the smarter they become. Grandma Mary thinks too many adults get annoyed with kids' questions. They tell kids lots of reasons why they can't answer their questions. "I'm busy" is the most common, but Grandma Mary has heard too many excuses that have led her to believe that too many parents simply don't know how to answer their children's questions, or they think that their child doesn't need to know certain information. Well, Grandma Mary has always told Skye that she could ask her absolutely anything, because if her mind asks the question, then she is old enough to hear an answer that can be worded appropriately for children. Grandma Mary has always enjoyed answering Skye's questions; even the hard ones, and Grandma Mary knew that Skye was going to ask her questions about her life that would bring back memories that she had kept buried for so very long.

Ever since Ms. Shumsky talked to Skye's class about the hardships her relatives faced during the Holocaust, Skye has been more interested in people's personal stories. Last week, Skye asked Grandma Mary to tell her about her life story, and she told Skye that she would ask her mom if she could stay over Friday night and return Saturday evening. She would tell Skye her story on Saturday. Her thoughts came to an end as she drove up to the curb of Skye's school.

"Hi, Grandma Mary," Skye yelled. She was more excited than usual, because she was going to spend Friday and Saturday with Grandma Mary and Grandpa Marv. She threw her backpack and duffle bag in the back seat. The bag included things to wear, things for fun, and her toothbrush. "What are we going to do today, Grandma Mary?" Skye asked.

"Well, if you want to do something together, we can work on this brand-new puzzle I just bought, or we can knit, or possibly read together on the side porch. It looks like the rain is going to come down soon. Or you can always do your artwork, alone. I bought you some new art supplies when I purchased the new puzzle," Grandma Mary said. As Skye pulled the puzzle out of the art supply bag, she studied the picture of two beautiful horses with a big red barn behind them on the cover of the box. Still deciding on what she would do, Skye looked in the bag and then screamed with joy. Grandma Mary had bought her a much larger box of colored pencils and a bigger drawing pad. "Grandma Mary, I love the puzzle, but I love the art supplies even more. I've decided I'm going to draw." Grandma Mary smiled and replied, "That's great to hear."

Skye cleared the space on the table after her snack of sweet mango and unsweetened, decaffeinated iced tea, then she grabbed Grandma Mary's bird book. She planned to draw Grandma Mary's three favorite birds; a cardinal, a blue jay, and a robin. Skye was shocked when she heard Grandma Mary announcing that dinner was ready. Looking up at the clock in disbelief, Skye realized she had been drawing for over two hours! "Okay, Grandma Mary," Skye replied as she began packing her new colored pencils into the box. When finished, Skye walked into the kitchen with her large drawing pad to show Grandma Mary her progress. Grandma Mary loved Skye's drawings. "I'm going to give this to you when I'm done," said Skye as she displayed her unfinished birds. Skye thought this would be a nice gift for Grandma Mary, to show just how thankful she was for the new supplies. "Thank you, Skye!" I will buy a beautiful frame and find a special place to hang it once you're finished," said Grandma Mary as she admired her granddaughter's hard work. Skye put the drawing pad away for later and helped Grandma Mary clear and set the table for dinner. Skye and Grandma Mary were having veggie burgers with lettuce, tomato, and onions, some sweet potato fries, and a large glass of water for dinner tonight.

However, Grandpa Marv grabbed a bowl for some cereal, a banana, and a glass of water for his meal. Skye giggled as she watched Grandpa Marv gather the items for his dinner. As he sat at the table, Skye looked over at Grandma Mary and commented, "Well, at least Grandpa Marv is eating some healthy granola cereal, Grandma." They all laughed. As they sat around the table together, Skye talked about her day at school.

Once they finished dinner, Grandma Mary reminded Skye of the next day's planned events and said, "We have a very full day tomorrow, so you need to spend a relaxing evening in your room." Since its Friday, that meant that Skye didn't have homework, so she's happy she gets to choose between knitting, reading, or watching one TV program.

The sunshine woke Skye. She got up and could hear her grandparents talking downstairs. She ran downstairs and greeted them with kisses and hugs. "What are we doing today?" Skye asked as she pulled the chair from under the table. Grandma Mary began with, "First, we are going to have a very light meal because I am taking you to my yoga class. So, once you finish, I want you to go upstairs and put your gym clothes on and we'll meet at the SUV in about 20 minutes." Skye loved the yoga studio. The floors were heated, the walls were white brick, and the instructor was very nice. Grandma Mary advised Skye not to worry about keeping up with the poses, because the class is "slow flow" and will consist of new participants and easy to follow relaxing exercise. Once they arrived, Grandma Mary gave Skye a mat and a water bottle. The instructor was so much fun and Skye enjoyed the movement and breathing exercises. Yoga made Skye feel peaceful. When they got home, Grandma Mary gave Skye the rest of her meal, and they went upstairs to her special study. She and Skye never talked in there before, so Skye thought this must be a serious talk.

After Skye settled on a floor cushion and Grandma Mary in her chaise lounge, the **Wisdom Warrior** began, "Skye, Grandma Mary had a very tough childhood." With a loving and sincere voice, Grandma Mary told Skye how she was the second of eleven children. Her family was so poor that they were on welfare, a program where the government provides a family with free food. Grandma Mary said they never celebrated birthdays, and rarely celebrated Christmas or other holidays. One Christmas she got one doll to share with her sister and another Christmas her mother put up a tree after Christmas had passed. Grandma Mary explained that the family was sometimes without lights, or the electricity until her parents could come up with money to pay the bills. She also shared that the family would sometimes go to sleep without food, and that she didn't have a regular bed. Grandma Mary shared a mattress on the floor with a few younger siblings, and there were days where one might wet the bed; getting pee on her during the night. Grandma Mary couldn't remember a Thanksgiving when her family wasn't given a free turkey and other items to ensure they had something to eat on the holiday. Grandma Mary explained to Skye that many of the experiences she and her siblings suffered was the result of her parents not having jobs. "Grandma Mary, why didn't your parents work?" Skye asked. Grandma Mary explained that her parents were smarter than she. However, Grandma Mary's dad was an alcoholic and would drink constantly because he got tired of being rejected for jobs, he knew he was qualified for, simply because he was African American. She explained her mom's brain was damaged; she couldn't think clearly, and often had strange thoughts that the doctors couldn't fix. Grandma Mary went on to explain that the day her family was evicted and their belongings were put on the sidewalk, was the day she decided that she wouldn't be poor. Her childhood experiences sparked a strong desire in her to always do well in school; to fight for the knowledge and opportunities she deserved just as much as anyone else.

Grandma Mary described her neighborhood, referring to it as a "food desert," due to the absence of nearby grocery stores. In most cases, there were only corner stores with overpriced necessities, like toilet paper, and they had no access to healthy foods like fresh fruit and vegetables. There were lots of very bad surgery drinks and treats with toxic chemicals in them she said. Kids ate peeling lead paint from their home walls, and the lead in the water poisoned their brains, causing permanent learning problems. There were also billboards everywhere, advertising alcohol and cigarettes. Grandma Mary explained that once she understood strategic environments like these were another form of oppression, she decided she would not let racism break her. Grandma Mary finished her talk by telling Skye how social workers picked up all of her siblings when she was fifteen years old, and separated everyone into different foster homes. Skye's brain was filled with more emotions than questions, so she just listened.

"Wow, Grandma Mary, you don't look or act like you had such a hard life," sighed Skye. With a sense of accomplishment, Grandma Mary replied, "Yes, I know, Love. That's because I've made a good life for myself by getting my education, and becoming what I wanted to be in life." She went on to explain to Skye that people shouldn't look down on anyone, because no one truly knows one's story until they hear it from that very person. Everyone needs to have more love for the suffering." Relieved that she shared the hard, painful truth with her granddaughter, Grandma Mary says, "I think you've heard enough for today." Skye stood up and gave her Grandma Mary a long, big, tight hug; one without words, but lots of love.

As Grandma Mary took Skye home, she drove through a neighborhood like the one she was raised in and advised her, "You must never forget how fortunate you are Love. Whenever possible, help those who are less fortunate."

"How?" asked Skye. Grandma looked at Skye with a loving smile, "By always being the very kind girl that you are." Skye reassured Grandma Mary with, "I will." As she hugged Grandma Mary before she got out of the SUV, Skye said, "Grandma Mary, I really, really, really love you."

"And Grandma Mary loves you even more!" They gave each other a kiss and a long hug. Skye's mother was waiting for her at the opened front door. "Love you, mom," Madison yelled from the door. "Love you too, sweetheart," replied Grandma Mary. They blew each other kisses as Grandma Mary drove away.

Story 9 ███████████

Careers: Defining Moments

Skye and all her classmates were very excited about class today. Two weeks ago, Ms. Graham assigned the students to do reports on careers they wanted to have when they are adults. She introduced the lesson by telling students that they will probably have at least five careers in their lifetime, and that it wasn't too early to think about the careers that they are interested in. The students had glum looks on their faces, and the teacher knew that it was probably because they thought that she would make them do a report on five careers. "No, students," she said as she read their expressions. "You will only be choosing one job for your report. But I want you to be thinking of other jobs you might want to do during your long life." Sounds of relief could be heard around the room.

The students were very attentive when Ms. Graham gave directions for how they would complete their

78

report. She read from a paper that she passed out to all students.

"You will report on a career of your choice by defining it, and then answering what, how, and why questions about your job choice," she said. Skye figured that the "who" was left out because the paper is about her, and the "when" questions were left out because the paper is about her and her future job as an adult. Ms. Graham added, "Then you will pick a regular, or famous person, in the job you picked and write why you admire the person that you selected." She also told the class that the report had to be between one to two pages long. Finally, Ms. Graham told the students to bring in a picture of their career person for a presentation, that in all should last about five minutes.

"It is now time for us to start our reports," said Ms. Graham. Then the students cheered as Ms. Graham explained that the entire day would be dedicated to reports, and when the reports were completed, they could color, read, or talk quietly in the special group meeting place in the corner of the room that was filled with comfortable seat cushions. The students worked on the computers to complete their reports, then when they were done, they put their names on pieces of paper and put it in a box. Ms. Graham called up students in the order of the names she picked from the box.

The class found the reports very interesting. Students picked jobs as firemen, policemen, bakers, singers, web designers, computer engineers, computer hackers, photographers, doctors, nurses, teachers, astronauts, artists, graphic designers, and dentists.

Skye's career choice was interior design. She said that she wanted to work for herself after she was trained. Skye wanted to design homeless shelters and group homes for kids who didn't have foster homes. Five out of six black male students chose professional sports. Two picked professional basketball, two picked professional football, and one picked professional boxing. The sixth black male student chose to become a judge when he grew up.

Everyone was so polite during the reports until Jared presented his report. Everyone knew Jared was the smartest one in the class. He loved learning and he loved getting A's even more. Jared was a quiet person, but very confident in his own manner. As soon as Jared said what his career choice was, all of the other black boys began to snicker and laugh. As they covered their mouths to hide their smiles from laughter, one mumbled, "Jared made a stupid choice." The other four black boys looked puzzled, but Skye was mad. She liked Jared a lot. In fact, Jared was her favorite male friend in class. Ms. Graham reminded the students about proper behavior and said any future outbursts would mean after school detention with a written misbehavior referral. The boys settled down and stopped making noises, but they all continued occasionally looking at one another while rolling their eyes, as Jared continued his report. Luckily, Jared didn't seem to care what anyone thought, except Skye. She always supported him. He looked over at Skye when he was finished and she gave him the same broad smile that he gave her when she finished her report. Everyone had 45 minutes of free time before school ended. Skye thought to herself that this was a perfect way to spend a Friday, and now she has the weekend ahead.

Grandpa Marv was waiting for Skye when she came out of the building. As Skye climbed into the car, she excitedly told Grandpa Marv about how her report went, and about her other favorite reports. Suddenly, Skye's voice and demeanor changed; she told Grandpa Marv about how all her black boy classmates picked professional sports, except for Jared. She was clearly unhappy at the fact that the boys made fun of Jared as he presented his report. As she looked up at Grandpa Marv, she said "You don't look surprised, Grandpa Marv."

"That's because I'm not surprised," he replied. "How come you aren't surprised, Grandpa?" asked Skye. As Grandpa Marv backed his car into the driveway, he calmly stated, "We'll talk about it as we wash my car." As he winked at Skye, he added, "If you do a good job, I will pay you, then you can put the money in your money jar to save for something special."

"Okay, Grandpa Marv," said Skye, still a little puzzled with his response.

Grandpa Marv and Skye quietly ate their walnut brownie snack as they drank their almond milk. Then they went out to the driveway. Skye filled the blue bucket with water, while Grandpa Marv got the soap, Windex glass cleaner, paper towels, and hand vacuum. After filling the bucket, Skye ran downstairs to get lots of rags. "We can't wash the car until you put on the extra work clothes your Grandma Mary left for you." Skye forgot she still had her school clothes on, so she ran upstairs to change. It was a nice, hot day and Skye loved washing Grandpa's car on days like this, so she could get wet while washing the suds off with the hose. Grandpa Marv usually dried most of the car while she vacuumed the inside.

As they began washing the car, the **Wisdom Warrior** began, "Skye, too many of our black boys want to be professional athletes because those careers are advertised to them more than any other career opportunity. Because these kids see the drastic difference in the lives of those in sports and the men in their everyday lives, you don't blame them. A lot of the adult males in their lives are poor and unemployed because of an unequal education, and also because of the lack of job opportunities. Playing professional sports is a fine career choice, but the black males in your class need to learn some important lessons about who becomes a professional." As he reached to wash the top of the car, Grandpa Marv adds, "I am going to tell you a story about your uncle Bernie and my best friend Devon Smith. After I finish my story, I am going to have you give invitations to all of your black male classmates to come play basketball on your Uncle Bernie's hoop. I will ref the game myself and when the game is over, I am going to give them some snacks, and tell them the same story I'm telling you now."

Devon Smith and Grandpa Marv had been best friends since middle school. Luckily, Devon Smith had a college degree and a successful business career. He was a very talented athlete and played for a national football team following college. Devon was successful in his career for several years, until he got hurt. So, Grandpa Marv stressed that the first point of his story, was that only the very best athletes get to play pro sports. If they can't play anymore, they should have a back-up plan. A good education in a specific field *is* a good backup plan, added Grandpa Marv. He continued and explained that Skye's uncle Bernie wanted to play professional basketball.

Grandpa admitted Bernie was a very good player, but he knew deep inside that he didn't have the skills to be a professional. Grandpa Marv's next point was that just because someone wants something very badly, doesn't mean they have the skills to get it. Uncle Bernie even played Division 1 college basketball, but after one year of playing, he decided that the many hours of practice didn't leave him the time he needed to study. Bernie was studying to earn a degree in Sports Communication Media. He wanted to be a sports announcer; in fact, he was already working at a radio station on campus. Bernie had to take radio, television, and production courses for his college degree. To his surprise, he fell in love with production, and after years of hard work, ABC Sports hired him to work for them. He made lots of money, dressed like he belonged on a fashion magazine, and traveled the world. He was so talented at his job that he supervised many other employees. Bernie met and hung out with so many of his favorite pro athletes from every sport. He even covered a Super Bowl and National Football Championship game as leading producer!

Grandpa Marv ended his story with, "So Skye, your classmates need to know that if they don't play professional sports, they can still select a professional sport career like a sports agent, sports attorney, a position in sports management, or even a sports therapist."

As he hoses the suds off the car, while getting Skye wet, Grandpa Marv suggests, "This weekend we can make up invitations for your friends to come over to Uncle Bernie's the following Saturday around 1:00 P.M. Enjoying the fun, Skye yells, "Thanks, Grandpa! I can't wait to give them the surprise invitations."

Story 10 ████████

> *Our mistreatment was just not right, and I was tired of it.* Nelson Mandela

Racial Profiling: Expectations Unexpected

Grandma Mary put two big red apples into a small brown paper bag. She then filled two refillable water bottles with water and put them in her reusable tote bag. Grandma Mary wanted to do what she could to save the environment from all things plastic. It was Grandma Mary's turn to pick up Skye, and she decided that she was going to go to the sale at her favorite store, Marshalls. She pressed the remote to the garage, and put on her coat, grabbing her purse, and locking the front doors.

Grandma was running about ten minutes late because she was sitting on her second-floor porch reading a book when she saw two black women taking a walk with their children. Both children were unhappy about something and started to cry. Grandma Mary couldn't really hear what was wrong. One mother bent down and tried to reason with her child. The other mother slapped her child several times and told the child to be quiet. Grandma Mary thought to herself, how can you be quiet when you're in pain from someone hitting you? She didn't really like passing judgment on people's personal matters, but she noticed how spanking seemed to be the first choice of discipline, when there were other options.

Grandma Mary wondered if adults would like to be hit when they made mistakes. She knows she isn't perfect, after all, and she remembers giving Skye's mother, Madison a few frantic smacks on her bottom when she was three, only because she would grab her cleaning solution and put the bottle up to her mouth while she was watching her clean the bathroom. Looking back now, Grandma Mary knows she would have handled it differently today, even though she did it because she panicked, thinking Madison might have swallowed some of the cleaner. Grandma Mary liked to approach each day with the thought "When you know better, you do better." So, she was thinking of Stacey's Patton's article on spanking; that it explained African American parents spanking their children because it was passed down through slavery. White masters beat African American adults and children regularly. They even allowed their own children to beat slave children. Grandma Mary thinks black parents would reconsider spanking if they knew that their ancestors considered children sacred, and that modern spanking generally turns into beatings as children get older, often with the worst of consequences.

"Grandma Mary you're really late," said Skye as she climbed into the SUV. "I'm so sorry," said Grandma

Mary. "How come you're late?" Skye asked. Grandma Mary is usually on time, but she knew that there are always adults watching over the car riders, even in cases when parents are a few minutes late. "I was on my porch reading and watching people walk down the street, but lost track of time," she said to Skye as she drove away. "You're going the wrong way said Skye."

"No, I'm not," smiled Grandma Mary. "Your house is not this way," said Skye. "I know. Who said we are going to my house?" Now intrigued, Skye asks, "Where are we going?" "We're going to a sale at my favorite store. We'll have enough time to eat our snack as I drive there," Grandma Mary told Skye as she reached in her bag to grab the apple and water. "Will you buy me something, Grandma Mary?" Skye asked. "That's the plan. You deserve a special treat for being so wonderful," said Grandma Mary. "Thanks, Grandma Mary!" Skye said as she bit into her apple.

Grandma Mary grabbed a shopping cart and went directly to the clearance section for children. She told Skye that she could choose two clothing items from the long racks in front of them. As Skye sifted through the clothes packed tightly on the first rack, she found a cool pair of jeans and a gray tee with a big smile logo on it. Once Skye had made her selection, Grandma Mary headed toward the active section to look at the new yoga clothes on sale. She noticed that a woman seemed to be following them. Even though it appeared the woman was looking at clothing on the same racks, Grandma Mary became suspicious of her when she continued to appear in the same sections, she and Skye were shopping. The woman didn't leave until Grandma Mary put her selection in their cart. Suddenly, the woman appeared again in the towel section where Grandma Mary had just arrived. Now, Grandma Mary knew for sure the woman was following her. Grandma Mary noticed that the woman had no purse, no cart, and no salesperson's tag. She was obviously an undercover security guard. Grandma Mary looked around and noticed that while the store was quite crowded, there were no other people of color, except for her and Skye. Grandma Mary understood that several stores were losing money as a result of theft, but she also knew people didn't steal because of the color of their skin. They steal because of hardships, or because they don't value doing the right thing.

Trying desperately to maintain her composure, Grandma Mary finds herself remembering an incident with her best friend's daughter. Grandma Mary and Rachel, one of her best friends, were having tea, when her daughter Jenny came home from her first day on the job. Jenny was visibly upset as she told her mom that the store manager told her to follow any black people who came into their store because they were known to steal. "That's ridiculous! It made me so mad, mom!" Jenny further explained to her mom that the manager wasn't happy when Jenny asked her why would she agree to do something like that? Rachel beamed with pride, as she realized her daughter stood up for what was right. As Jenny continued her disgust at the situation, Grandma Mary thanked Jenny for taking a stand, and told her that speaking up might change the manager's mind, as well as prevent unfounded racial profiling.

Skye looked up at Grandma Mary and broke her memory saying, "I think that lady is following us." The lady heard Skye, and continued listening as

Grandma Mary responded saying, "You're right Skye. She *is* following us." The lady's face turned red. Grandma Mary continued, "Well, while she is watching you and I , other people whom she doesn't suspect of stealing, are taking things without paying for them, because they are very aware that she is too busy following *us*."

"I know Grandma Mary." "Why does she think we are stealing?"

"We'll talk about it on the way home. Your mother is expecting us soon, so we need to check out." They headed to the checkout and a black cashier called up a white woman next in line. The cashier gave the woman a big smile and made small talk, both laughing at something the woman said. Grandma Mary was next. She was expecting the same wide smile the woman in front of her received. Instead, the woman put her head down, her smile disappeared, and she rang up the items without a word. Grandma Mary paid her bill and asked the woman politely to call a manager to meet her at the front of the store. Grandma Mary knew she would be late dropping Skye off to her house, so Grandma Mary called her mom to let her know.

"May I help you?" the manager asked. "Yes, thank you. I just wanted you to know that I didn't enjoy my shopping experience in your store today. I am a regular customer at this location, but might not return after today," explained Grandma Mary. The manager, looking unconcerned, said "Yes, I see you in here all the time. How can I help?" So, Grandma Mary told her that she didn't appreciate being followed, and that the cashier was being rude for no reason at all. She didn't bother telling the manager that she felt the woman followed her because she held some false and negative views about black people.

After Grandma Mary spoke, the manger changed her attitude right away. The manager was very nice and appeared to be embarrassed by Grandma Mary and Skye's experience. The manager said she would warn the young cashier, and that she would speak with security. When she was leaving the store, the manager gave Grandma Mary a 30% off coupon to use on her next visit, in an effort to keep her as a valued customer. As the manager sincerely apologized, Grandma Mary thanked her for understanding her concerns and for the coupon.

On the way home Grandma Mary told Skye that racial profiling describes the incident of security following them, because they believe black people steal. Grandma then explained that she made it a point to speak with the manager, because racial profiling is illegal, and the manager should be held accountable. Security should be in the store to keep everyone safe and watch all customers. Grandma Mary shared Jenny's story with Skye to demonstrate how important it is for everyone to stand up for what's right. Grandma Mary also shared a story about Skye's mom, Madison. Grandma Mary explained that Madison went shopping with her friend Susan one afternoon years ago. Unfortunately, Madison ended up calling Grandpa Marv to pick her up because her friend Susan was caught stealing, and security was keeping both girls at the store until their parents came to pick them up. Grandma Mary said that when Madison came home from the store, she told her mom that she didn't believe in stealing and was afraid to do anything like it, and like how Grandma Mary and Skye experienced today, she was used to being followed in the stores. Her friend, Susan, was caught because the buzzer went off while the security was following Madison.

Skye proudly said, "Grandma Mary, I love when you let people know that you don't like when you're not being treated fairly." With a proud smirk, Grandma Mary said, "I know you do, and I see my ways are rubbing off on you." Grandma Mary went on to explain to Skye that if people talk to others respectfully, they can generally reason with them, and might even be surprised with more than what they expected. "Yes, like your 30% off coupon," said Skye.

"Exactly." said Grandma Mary.

As they pulled up to Skye's house, she thanked Grandma Mary for her clothes. Grandma replied, "You're welcome," as Skye got out of the SUV and ran up the stairs. Then they blew each other a kiss and waved goodbye.

Story *11*

The ability to read awoke inside of me some long dormant craving to be mentally alive.
Malcolm X

Reading:
Dr. Luke,
The Reading Warrior

Skye's new principal, Dr. Ivy, was very popular. It's been a month into the school year, and Skye and her classmates couldn't wait to go to school every day. He was Whitney Magnet Public School's first African American principal. Every morning, Dr. Ivy is always at the door to greet them with an enormous smile as they enter the school building, and when they leave to go home. He is very tall man with a fade haircut. Dr. Ivy wears a really cool suit almost every day. He would always walk the hallways or around the cafeteria making sure children find their way to class or are eating their food, instead of playing with it. He has made many changes to the way the school is run, but Skye's favorite is the morning ritual. Every day it starts with the PA announcements, and each day of the week begins differently. Word of the week, inspirational quotes, jokes, meaningful facts, and short inspirational passages, are five ways to begin

92

each day of the week. Volunteer students with motivating voices get to read the activities over the PA. Then the assistant principal makes brief general and special announcements. Today, he announces that the first assembly of the year is the last hour of the school day. Important short assemblies take place any day of the week, but regular assemblies take place the last Friday of every month. After the final announcements, all the teachers have the students close their eyes and take five deep breaths through their nose and out of their nose, and then after, think of one thing they are thankful for. Dr. Ivy has the teachers show the students the breathing exercises because it also calms the students, that combined with positive thinking, the students can focus solely on school, and not have to think about the hardships that they deal with at home.

Today is a regular assembly day. All the students walk quietly into the auditorium and when all students are seated, Ms. Wilson, the school librarian, introduces the speaker for the first assembly of the year. The speaker is sitting in a chair near the podium that Ms. Wilson is standing at. She introduces Professor Luke, and explains that he is called Dr. Luke, because he has the highest degree that you can earn in an educational career. The students applaud as Dr. Luke walks to the podium. Dr. Luke is tall, handsome, and the color of dark chocolate. He is wearing a shiny light gray suit, white shirt, a red tie with tiny white polka dots, and black shiny loafers. "Thank you for the introduction," he says to Ms. Wilson as he stands at the podium. The students noticed immediately that Dr. Luke has an accent. It is clear and smooth like music. Dr. Luke had them all stand, touch their toes, reach tall, bend to the right and left, and then he told them to take a seat. The students figured out that Dr. Luke had them do those few movements so that they would be able to sit still and listen to his talk.

"Students, I am here to talk to you about my very favorite activity in life. You can probably guess what that is since the librarian introduced me. So, I want everyone to say what that activity is at once," opened the speaker. Once he counted down to three, the audience yelled out, "Reading!"

"Precisely," he cheered, with victory pumps to the air. Then Dr. Luke turned on his laptop and a large map of Africa appeared. He said he is from Sierra Leone, West Africa, and pointed to it on the map. He then showed them many beautiful scenes from his country, as well as pictures of famous natural resources. Dr. Luke told them he wished he had more time to tell them about his beautiful country, its people and resources, but his talk today is about reading, because he said that he considers it the most valuable resource of all.

"Africans have always been famous for their oral stories, with lessons passed down from generation to generation," he said. Dr. Luke talked about the famous African folktales that students still read today. He also talked about how African stories are different from American stories. "African stories skip all around, trying to keep you focused or entertained. American stories usually start with a beginning, then the middle, and finally the end." And then Dr. Luke's tone turned serious. "During slavery, slaves were not allowed to read or write, and had to suffer all forms of torture if they were caught reading. So, I want you to think for a few moments, why were slaves not permitted to read.

"Why do you think that was true?" Dr. Luke said. "Slave owners didn't want slaves to be smart, especially smarter than them," yelled Skye."

"Yes!" Dr. Luke said, searching the audience for the wise voice. Then Jameel belted out, "The owners knew slaves would be able to do things on their own."

"They knew they could escape easier," said Jared. "Great answers!" exclaimed Dr. Luke. "All of you touched on my main point, that the masters knew that it would be very difficult to control a smart man or woman." He went on to explain that the most important point he wanted to make, is that if learning to read caused slaves to be tortured or killed, then the owners knew knowledge was the most valuable skill to be had. He asked the audience, "By a show of hands, tell me who likes to read?" Less than half the students raised their hand.

Not surprised at the response, Dr. Luke asked, "How many of you select the first thing you see when you go clothes shopping? Not waiting for a response, he said, "Silly, right?" He went on to tell the audience that it is silly to say that one doesn't like to read. He said that shopping is like reading, one must look around until they find the perfect book. There are books about absolutely anything, and everything you love, as well as famous people you want to know more about. Librarians love to help you find the perfect book. If you fail to learn some of life's lessons found in books, you might be taken advantage of in life because you don't know the truth about things.

You can't get all of your answers from the Internet, added Dr. Luke. "Critical cultural information is missing from your school textbooks, so you need to read about it on your own," encouraged the professor.

He guaranteed that if the students read about their culture, no one could ever make them feel inferior, because they would know the truth about their own greatness.

"When we read about other cultures, we will come to understand, appreciate, respect, and value other people." He asked the audience, "Don't you think it would be boring to live in a world where all the people were the same?" We should want information about different cultures as much as we desire foods influenced by other cultures, as well as clothing styles from other cultures." He explained that a person can't truly know who they are without learning about themselves. "Reading makes you so smart, and helps you to excel in all that you do in your journey in life." As Dr. Luke began to wrap up his presentation, all of the students stood and chanted, "Read us a story!" and Dr. Luke read a story about how reading changed his life. The students jumped up from their seats when he finished, and gave Dr. Luke thunderous applause.

Skye could hardly control her joy. She practically leaped into the car. "Grandpa Marv, today was my very favorite assembly ever!"

"Wow," said Grandpa. "I think I'll put the air on today because you are so full of energy you might fly out the window!" He added.

"That's very funny, Grandpa!" Skye said as she told Grandpa Marv about the speaker who came from the same country as Grandma Mary's father. She told Grandpa Marv almost everything he said, word for word. "Grandpa, the kids thought he was handsome and hilarious. He dressed as nice as you when you wear your suits."

"Thank you, Brown Sugar," he said.

"Grandpa, I think he convinced the kids that reading is very important and fun. He didn't talk about the comics though, but Grandma Mary said you learn from *anything* you read. She said when you have to figure out anything, that when you read, you are getting smarter. Grandma Mary even convinced me to read what I don't like because she told me no matter how much I don't want to read something the teacher gives me, if I try to figure out what I was supposed to learn, I will be happy that I learned something new. She is right. One day, we had to read about polymers and I didn't want to read about a word that sounded boring. But after I read the information, I learned that polymers are plastics, and plastics are destroying our planet. That's why Grandma Mary and mom have stopped using plastic as much."

Skye talked from the moment she got in the car, and didn't stop even after she walked into Grandpa Marv's house. "Skye, you are usually starving after school and can't wait to eat your snack. You've been talking for 45 minutes," said Grandpa Marv as he hung his hat. "Forty- five minutes!" He said again, as he pointed to the kitchen clock. "You've had a very interesting day, but if you don't eat your snack now, you won't have energy to do your homework when you get home."

97

"You're right Grandpa Marv. I'm starving," said Skye, realizing that today she was more excited than hungry. She laughed at herself.

Skye finally stopped talking as she devoured the peanut butter crackers and drank the almond milk Grandpa Marv sat out for her. "As soon as you've finished your snack, I want you to meet me outside by the car. It will be time to take you home," Grandpa Marv said as he headed out to water the flowers in the front yard. "Okay," replied Skye.

"Ready, Grandpa," Skye said coming out of the front door with her backpack. A few minutes later, Grandpa Marv was waking Skye up as they pulled up to her house. She had worn herself out from all the excitement of her day.

Story 12

> *Injustice anywhere is a threat to justice everywhere.* Martin Luther King Jr.

Police: Blame is NOT the Name of Your Game

While sitting on the couch, in front of the warm fire, Grandma Mary is knitting a sweater for Skye. While it's early May, the temperature still has a winter chill. Unconsciously knitting, while staring at the low flickering flames, Grandma finds herself thinking about one of her favorite professors from college, Professor Douglas. The one statement he would always revisit in his lectures was, "People in power often blame the victim for causing their own problems." Grandma Mary rests her knitting in her lap as several tears fall from her face. She is thinking of the death of a young black boy in Cleveland, Ohio, who was killed by police. She didn't know Tamir Rice, but according to African tradition, ancestors say that we should treat all children as if they are our own; to watch over and protect them as if we are one

99

enormous extension of our family. According to the news, Tamir was playing with a toy gun and was shot and killed within seconds by a police officer driving up to the playground. Grandma Mary is disgusted by what she feels are completely false accounts, that the policeman gave for his hasty decision to kill young Tamir. She's even more upset that the officer will suffer no consequence for taking the life of a precious and innocent child. She begins to think of all the black men and women that she hears about on the news that are killed daily. Grandma Mary knows that there are so many more that lose their lives, that we normally don't hear about. In most of the cases, the police blame the victims for reasons that don't make sense, even when the video clearly shows that the police involved were not telling the truth.

It upsets Grandma Mary when so many white people are outraged when black people fight to have dishonorable police men punished, which according to the law, need a consequence for the loss of the precious lives of so many of their people. There are dishonorable people in all professions. She believes that people who think all policemen are honorable don't want to face the truth, or they don't value the lives of all the people that the police took an oath to protect and serve. Some people even think all policemen are honorable, simply because they wear a uniform. Grandma Mary feels that the slogan *Blue Lives Matter* was created in response to *Black Lives Matter*, to let black people know that police lives matter more than black lives. The *Black Lives Matter* slogan was created from unbearable grief because police were getting away with killing so many black people, mostly for unjust reasons, and with no consequences. Policemen who do not value black life, as much as they value their own, should not be policemen she mumbled to herself. Then she put down her knitting and decided to do some chores. She is very grateful that the Whitney Magnet Public School will have a workshop on Saturday for parents and students, to discuss the police and the black community.

It is Saturday, and there is only room to stand in the Whitney Magnet Public Auditorium. There are mostly African American people there, but there are also many white faces in the crowd as well. This fact brings a smile to Grandma Mary's face, because *all* people need to fight for justice. Skye sees her classmate Melissa and her parents across the room and waves. Skye is sitting with her parents and grandparents. On stage are several people sitting at a long table. At the table are a black and white policeman, Dr. Ivy was in the middle, the head of the parent PTA at Whitney, and a diversity expert. The moderator is Ms. Clemens of the local NAACP. She introduced herself and stated that this event was a proactive attempt to fill in the community on actions taken by the police department to assure that their department will serve and protect all citizens in particular- the children. She said everyone at the table will speak to a specific theme. When the final speaker is finished, people from the audience could ask questions.

Dr. Ivy came to the podium first. He thanked the speakers and Ms. Clemens for sponsoring the event, and then he thanked all the parents for the standing room only attendance. "We are all one family and we will protect our family by learning what is necessary to keep all of us safe and happy in our community,"

101

said Dr. Ivy. Ms. Thomas, the PTA President, was next. She read the concerns parents discussed at the last parent meeting. The list included things like improved police training, regular contact with the community; to get to know the people living there, educating young people on how to respond to police in hostile situations, jobs, and other activities to keep the area of young people out of trouble. Most importantly, the parents want everyone in the community to really look out for each other.

Two police officers, one white and the other black, came up after Ms. Thomas finished at the podium. Each officer spoke to the fact that they didn't see any changes necessary for their department and felt their police department was doing their best. There were a few groans from the audience, because many knew that one can't change what one refuses to see. The parent representative spoke after the officers. She listed several concerns, but the main one was that many parents felt the police didn't respect or understand the youth in the community. The final speaker was the diversity expert. Ms. Thomas said that while she appreciated the hard work of the police department, today's response made it clear that the department was not in sync with the community, because they truly didn't understand all the people they were hired to protect and serve. She said the police would receive training to address unconscious bias of both white and black police, and even from living in a country where people of color have always been seen in a negative light. Ms. Thomas talked about how so many in the community have been discriminated against and blamed for conditions that they did not create. She said bias kills when policemen view black male children as adults. She ended by saying no culture compares themselves to the worst in their culture, and that the police should be trained to recognize bias that sees all black people as criminals.

Most of the questions for the panel were directed to the police. The police said that children should not play with toy guns because too many guns look real. Children need to know they might lose their life if the police think the gun is real. Then they listed several warnings to the adults in the audience. Keep both hands in full view on the steering wheel. Wait for directions from the police, and then let them know that you need to reach in a pocket, glove compartment or wherever else, for the information they request. Remain calm as you ask questions. Do not use profanity. Do not antagonize them even if you think you were unfairly stopped. By all means, go to court to plead your case if you feel the officer is in the wrong.

When the meeting was over, Skye and her parents followed Grandma Mary and Grandpa Marv to their house. They all sat in the living room to discuss the meeting. "Skye, tell us what you thought of the meeting?" her mom asked. She added, "We want you to ask all of your questions, and when you're done, we will discuss your concerns as a family." Skye looked at everyone and said, "I don't understand why the police have to be taught how to treat people. Why did they become police officers if they don't want to treat people fairly? I don't think it's fair that we can't shoot water pistols for fun on a hot day. Why do children have to be afraid that the police might hurt them? How come police have to be told on how to get to know us? How can they not know how to treat us, when we are just like their children, but we belong to a different culture or community? How come they don't see that it is mostly us who they are treating badly? And, how come they don't seem to really care about us? All of the speakers seemed really serious about helping solve the problem, but the two policemen didn't seem to think there really is a problem." Once she finished with her questions, Skye took a deep breath, feeling relieved to get all of her thoughts out in the open.

All the adults made eye contact and beamed with pride at the outstanding questions Skye asked. Grandma Mary began, "Well, first of all, young lady, I think you might want to seriously think about becoming a lawyer." Everyone firmly agreed. Skye said that she had already thought about it when she read a book about Thurgood Marshall in school. With a delighted smile, Madison, Skye's mom said, "Well Skye, the answer that answers most of your questions is simply our country has never really openly talked about equality for "all men and women," nor has it truly owned up to its responsibility in creating a system that deliberately discriminates against people of color. The system promotes mostly negative images of people of color, to make white people think they are superior." Skye's mom explained that police officers, whether black or white, who agree with the negative views, simply won't treat people of color fairly when we come into contact with them. She reminds Skye, "Remember when I told you some people of color also tend to accept negative images portrayed about themselves? And remember we also talked about how adults and children are being educated on history that does not include the contributions of people of color? Sweetie, I know it's grossly unfair, but it is reality for now. Just know that there will always be good people from all cultures, fighting for what is right,"

"I understand," said Skye. "I was so happy to see my friend Melissa and her parents there," she said remembering the more pleasant experiences from tonight's meeting. "Yes," said Grandpa Marv. "It is great when people want to do the right thing. And the more others want to do the right thing, the closer we will be to becoming a country of greatness, for all people. Right now, however, it is great for only *some* people," he concluded.

Grandma Mary said," Let's all go out to dinner," and everyone voted to go to Skye's favorite restaurant.

Story 13

> *We know through painful experience that freedom is never voluntarily given by the oppressor; it must be demanded by the oppressed.* Martin Luther King Jr.

Justice:
Peace in Justice

Skye runs in her grandparents' home after school. She hangs her backpack on the hook, removes her shoes, and slips on the grip socks Grandma Mary bought her so she doesn't slip on parts of the wood floors not covered with Grandma Mary's pretty area rugs. She then rushes to the dining table to see what snack Grandpa Marv has for her today. "Yummy!" Skye says as she drinks the unsweetened mango juice and eats her chocolate covered nuts.

As Skye sits at the table, she notices Grandpa's newspaper, on the table. Skye loves to read and by now, knows most of the words in the articles in Grandpa's paper. Today's paper had a large picture on the front page with a black man on the ground with a sign reading *No Justice, No Peace*. There was an angry looking white lady staring down at him, while one white policeman was kicking him, and another white officer was pointing a gun toward the protester as he was lying on the ground. The protesting black man was still holding a protest sign in his hand that read "No Justice, No Peace." Grandpa Marv has told Skye that he doesn't want her trying to read all that negative stuff in the paper. He usually lets her look at the pictures because he knows Skye loves to see if she can tell what the story is about by what's in the photo. Grandpa Marv walks into the dining room from the kitchen to join Skye at the table. She has often heard her parents and other adults talk about how black people are treated unfairly following news stories that were on TV, or from reading an article like the one in today's paper. Skye tries not to think about it too much because it makes her sad. As Grandpa Marv settled into his chair, Skye remembered what he said once. "If we ignore or pretend the bad things aren't happening to people of color, then the bad things will continue to happen." She recalled how he explained that it is up to brave people, Black, White, Latino, Asian, and all other ethnicities, to face injustice, and fight for people's rights by protesting peacefully. He said this would help make the bad people follow the law that says "…all men are created equal under the law."

"Grandpa, this picture in today's paper makes me feel sad," Skye stated. Glancing over at the paper, Grandpa Marv reminded Skye, "I thought I told you not to read those types of articles in the paper." Skye replied, "I didn't read the article Grandpa. I was just looking at the pictures like you told me I could." Understanding he couldn't always protect Skye from all the horrible things in the world, he knew as

Wisdom Warriors, he and Grandma Mary had to help Skye make sense of it all. To allow himself some time to think of the best way to discuss the article with Skye, Grandpa Marv said, "Why don't you go put your shoes on so we can walk down the street to the park. We can feed the ducks as we discuss the photo and any questions you have about it." Skye thought that Grandpa Marv didn't really feel like answering her questions today, so she said to him,

"Grandpa Marv we can talk about the newspaper another day, if you don't want to talk about it today." Impressed by Skye's thoughtfulness, Grandpa Marv explained, "No, Skye. Today is fine. As I've told you in the past, it's normal to feel sad when you see bad things happen to people for no reason, other than the color of their skin. In fact, it makes me sadder when you feel sad about bad things that shouldn't be happening anymore. Every day, your questions remind me that I, your Grandma Mary, your mom Madison, and your dad Melvin, have to help you find ways to feel better, and to always look for ways to solve these types of problems; to make life better for everyone."

Grandpa Marv sat on the bench reading his paper as Skye fed the ducks. When she finished, she sat next to Grandpa Marv and put her head on his shoulder. Grandpa Marv put the paper down and gave her a big hug. He put his arm around her as he began to answer her earlier questions, "Skye, there are lots of good policemen. One of Grandpa's very best friends is a policeman, and Grandma Mary's sister was one too. But there are bad policemen, too, like the ones in the picture. They are treating that man that way because they don't respect him, or anyone of color." Grandpa Marv explained that he didn't know exactly why those policemen don't respect people of color, but he said he could make a good guess. He said that they probably grew up around adults who said bad things about black people, who never lived around black people, or never really had any black friends; but most of all, they didn't learn in school how special the black culture is and how it only adds to the rich history of America. Grandpa Marv advised Skye not to worry because there are always good people fighting for what's right.

"Skye, everyone in America, has come from somewhere else. In fact, the Native Americans were the first people to come to America. Everybody else, including white people, lived in other countries before coming to America. Most people don't know, or choose to ignore, the truth about our American history. Most black people lived in Africa before they were brought here, against their wills, hundreds of years ago. Unlike other cultures in America who came to seek a better life, Africans were forced to come here to work as slaves by white Europeans. These people who only thought of the slaves as property, and not men, women, or children, disrespected and tortured them in so many cruel ways that I think you're still too young to discuss in detail. Slaves worked for free from sunrise to sunset; having to pick and harvest the cotton and tobacco crops, and were responsible for building some very important buildings that still exist today, like the White House."

"Wow, Grandpa, I didn't know that!" Skye said with surprise. Grandpa Marv went on to tell Skye, "While we all still suffer with prejudice treatment today, it doesn't compare to the treatment of black slave children back then. The slaves fought very hard to be free. It is because they didn't give up, that our culture is still around today. They are our true heroes." "When people say things like, *go back where you came from*, in this day and time, Skye, they forget that America is their home, just like it is theirs also. We don't want to go back to somewhere we've never lived, any more than they want to leave America to go back to Europe," explained Grandpa Marv. Africa is so enormous, that three maps of the United States can fit inside the map of Africa. Like many places, it has lots of very beautiful vegetation and mountains, with tons of resources that our country buys from them.; things like diamonds and gasoline are exported in mass quantities. Many places in Africa have cities with beautiful tall buildings that look like ours. Africans are beautiful people that come in all shades. They are brilliant people. Today, some Africans have come to this country to go to American colleges, and they even work in the best career fields. Africans are very proud people, and I believe that if African Americans learned of their true history, they would love and embrace Africa and their beautiful culture, too."

"Thanks, Grandpa. Every time you tell me stories about our ancestors, I love myself even more." Grandpa Marv smiled and told Skye, "The more information we have about ourselves, the more we will love ourselves, and each other. And the more information others learn about our culture and ancestors, they will love us too." Grandpa Marv added, "While that picture was hard for you to process Skye, the protester is right in saying, that we must have justice to live peacefully."

Story 14 ████████████

I've learned that people will forget what you said, people will forget what you did, but people will never forget how you made them feel. Maya Angelou

Ms. Graham: Power in Praise

It's been four weeks into the new school year, and Skye isn't enjoying school the way she used to. Until now, Skye liked all of her teachers. They were all very different, but all had made learning fun. Her favorite teachers so far were Ms. Drake and Ms. Bell. Ms. Drake was young and black and very athletic. Ms. Drake was always talking about eating right and exercising in between teaching her students. She was also a runner. Sometimes she would come out during recess time to organize relay races for kids who wanted to race. Skye would always join because running was her very favorite exercise. Ms. Drake didn't come out as often as Skye wished, because that's when she was planning or having a conference with parents. Ms. Bell was an older white woman.

She was always smiling and referring to her students as her children. Ms. Bell didn't like sports, but she loved to draw. Ms. Bell even asked Skye to draw holiday pictures on the whiteboard, because the art teacher told Ms. Bell about Skye's talent for drawing cartoon and fashion pictures.

Skye's new teacher Ms. Graham, doesn't like her at all. She tried to think of something nice about Ms. Graham, because her mom told her that no one is all bad, but she couldn't. She thought so hard it made her brain hurt. Ms. Graham is white. She isn't young, but she isn't old., and she is very mean. She seems very unhappy, and it seems she wants all her students to be unhappy too. No laughing was an unwritten rule.
Ms. Graham didn't explain lessons well either. She would get mad at students when they didn't understand her lessons. When most of the class failed a test, she told the class it is because she is a tough teacher and they would have to study more. Skye knew that her grades wouldn't improve by studying information that she didn't understand. Lots of kids were not doing well. Skye was passing, but her mostly A grades from past years, were now mostly B's and C's, and she used to love answering questions, but now only just listens to the lessons. Her other teachers would call on her when she raised her hand and when she didn't expect it. Ms. Graham ignored certain kids altogether, including her. Skye had a feeling she knew why Ms. Graham ignored certain kids and she would talk about her feelings today with Grandpa Marv when he picked her up after school.

School was over and Skye looked out for Grandpa's black Honda. Skye ran to the car and jumped in. "Hi

Grandpa!" What are we doing today?" Skye asked. "So, I feel like some ice cream today," Grandpa Marv said. So, I was thinking about going to the ice cream parlor, unless you want to go home and have Grandma Mary's rice cakes, hummus, and lemon water?" Skye burst out laughing. "I want ice cream," she grinned. Grandpa Marv pulled into his favorite custard store and ordered a double scoop of pecan ice cream. Skye ordered a chocolate turtle made with caramel, nuts, strawberries, vanilla custard and hot fudge. They ate their treat in the car because there weren't any seats left in the parlor. Neither of them spoke as they ate their ice cream. "Well, Brown Sugar, time to go," he said, as they both finished their treat at the same time. Grandpa's house was only a few blocks away, so Skye would wait until she was in the house to ask Grandpa Marv her question.

"Grandpa, I need to talk to you about something," Skye said. "Good, he said, because I have something, I want to talk to you about." "Okay," Skye said, having no idea what Grandpa Marv had on his mind. "I will go first," Grandpa Marv said. Grandpa's face turned serious. "Your mom tells me that your grades have dropped. She thought school might be a little harder for you this year, but I think it is something else because you are generally excited to talk about your day or ask for help if you need it."

"I don't like school anymore," she said. "My teacher is very mean. She's mean to everybody, but she is more mean to the black kids. She ignores us, doesn't call on us, and makes fun of our answers when they're wrong. Sometimes, she sends one of us to the principal's office for talking back, and she never sends a white kid out when they do the same thing."

"Have you told your mom about this?"

"No, I just told her she is mean."

"Well, you need to tell your mom exactly what you told me. Your mom needs to speak to Ms. Graham in a conference. Now it's your turn."

"What do you need to talk to me about?"

"The same thing," Skye said. "Well, if it's true, then that means that Ms. Graham is prejudice. We might not be able to do anything about how she chooses to feel, but we can make sure that she is fair to her students by letting her know how we feel. Now go grab the comics and let us read our favorites together."

Two days later, Skye's mom and Skye met Ms. Graham during Skye's recess time. Skye's mom began stating the problem and then she turned to Skye and to have her tell Ms. Graham about all the confusing things that have happened, to have her think that Ms. Graham was prejudice. Skye's mom had her write down main words on a card beforehand so that she wouldn't forget anything. Ms. Graham listened and when Skye finished, she said, "Look,

Ms. Carew. I don't see color." Very politely, Skye's mother said "then you don't see me or your black students." "If you don't see our black skin then we are invisible to you. And if you don't truly see your black students, then you also don't realize when you aren't treating them fairly." Then Skye's mom told Skye to step outside so that they could continue the conference in private.

On the way home Skye's mom said that Ms. Graham said she will try very hard to be more fair, and that Skye needed to do her part to do her best work, because the best way to respond to people who treat you as if you're invisible, is to visibly stand out with high grades. "Skye, she said, there are too many people in our country who think black students aren't the same as white students. This is because they never learned in their history classes that all cultures are different, but just as smart and worthy of fairness as any other culture. Don't ever give anyone permission to make you feel less than just because of their false beliefs. I expect you to get your best grades, and to not give Ms. Graham permission to think that you aren't as intelligent as you are. It is a fact of life that you will probably have more teachers who think like Ms. Graham, but you will also have more teachers like Ms. Bell and Ms. Drake. If you don't find much joy in your present class, find even more joy in learning because that is the main reason you are in school. School prepares you for very special careers for when you are an adult."

Skye looked at her mom and said, "I have an idea, mom." "What Love?" she said.

"I think I need to tell my black classmates what you just told me about getting good grades, and the other things my grandparents talk to me about. And I will start by telling them a nice thing about Ms. Graham." Mom asks , "What is that?"

"Ms. Graham said she would try very hard to be fair."

Mom looked at Skye and said, "I am so very proud to be your mom."

115

Story 15

Black Males in Special Ed: Empowerment From Within

As the last PTA meeting ended, Ms. Wilson, the organization's president, requested that the parents in attendance come up with ideas for ongoing problems that need to be addressed. She reminded the parents that problems are often easy to identify, but possible solutions serve as starting points to build on. Since Dr. Ivy's had forged an educational partnership with the parents, they have felt empowered to play an active role in addressing some of the problems the previous administration passed down to him. While Skye's parents, Madison and Melvin, regularly attend the meetings, Grandma Mary and Grandpa Marv are also regular participants. Madison's parents both had

116

careers in education, Grandma Mary, a teacher and Grandpa Marv, a retired guidance counselor. The family shares in making sure they provide first-hand information to one another when one of them can't attend. Other parents have also developed alliances to make sure they stay informed about issues and activities affecting their children. Jay's mom and Jared's mom became friends at one of the meetings, and now they take turns watching each other's children while one of them attends the meeting. Both parents are thrilled that childcare is no longer a cause for either of them to miss out on important information.

Melvin, Skye's dad, Grandpa Marv and Grandma Mary are on duty tonight, since Madison stayed home to help Skye with her homework, a project for school. Madison is thrilled that her parents show so much interest in Skye and her education, far beyond the usual grandparent.

Ms. Wilson called the meeting to order. She requested that all parents pass their suggestions and solutions up to the front of the room, where a volunteer was positioned to write each of them on a white board. When all papers were collected and read off one-by- one, Ms. Wilson assured all parents that all of their concerns would be addressed; however, the group agreed to focus on the large number of African American males in Whitney Magnet Public's Special Education classes. Other suggestions that were listed included establishing alternative consequences of detention for misbehavior, better teacher student communication, changes to the confusing report card comment section, and for a change in the conference days and times.

Ms. Wilson invited Mr. Carew, Grandpa Marv, up to the front to present some facts in reference to the problem, and to present his proposed solution. He thanked the parents for being in attendance, and paid special tribute to the three teachers who were there to represent the teaching staff. Grandpa Marv advised the audience that he was not only a concerned grandparent, but was a retired guidance counselor with first-hand experience. To ensure the parents understood the seriousness of the issue, he distributed statistics as he began his discussion.

Grandpa Marv started with the fact that special education classes across the nation mostly consist of African American male students. He explains that this fact is concerning because African Americans make up just 13% of the American population, yet they represent some of the largest numbers of dropouts, unemployed, and lowest paid in the job market. "The cycle begins right here in school," explained Grandpa Marv. He stated that several of these students suffer from a negative view of themselves. Grandpa Marv was happy to glance over to see diversity among the teacher representatives who were busily taking notes. He went on to explain that the lack of black role models as teachers was noted as a determining factor. He added that the color-blind approach, ignores black students. When educators say they don't see color, it reaffirms that they don't see their African American students. Grandpa Marv advised the teachers and audience that failing to acknowledge these black young men's uniqueness, only confirms they don't see or value their cultural differences. He highlighted some of the printed facts from the paper that was distributed, citing biased teacher recommendations and tests questions, as well as textbooks that were insensitive to their cultural values, and often suggesting their lack of intelligence and tendency toward violence.

Grandpa Marv wanted to ensure that the parents had a clear idea of who these Special Education students were, and the challenges they face every day when they come to school. Both Grandpa Marv and Grandma Mary wanted to do everything they could to help Dr. Ivy and the parents of Whitney Magnet Public School, to become the very best elementary school in Brooklyn. Based on his past career experience, Grandpa Marv knew the students enrolled in the Special Education program were not being prepared to successfully enter society. He didn't want these students to end up like so many dropouts who get lost in the education system.
"Nearly 80% of African American males in prison are high school dropouts," stated Grandpa Marv. Once Grandpa Marv presented all of the information and facts, he suggested implementing empowerment activities throughout school assignments. He stressed the importance of making the students feel good about themselves, and to reaffirm that they mattered. Pointing out the facts from his distributed information, Grandpa honed in on the fact that some of the Special Education students were very intelligent young boys, who were put in the program simply for misbehaving. Special Education programs were designed for students who have special educational needs due to learning difficulties, physical disabilities or behavioral problems. The entire room seemed surprised when he showed that most of the students in their program didn't fit those criteria. Grandpa Marv stated that it was important that each parent play a role in the solution, by talking

to their children on a daily basis, and remaining involved in their education by attending conferences, and not being afraid to confront racial issues when present.

Ms. Wilson thanked Mr. Carew for his in-depth report and prepared to call the meeting to a close. However, before she did, most parents voted for the next concern to be discussed at the next meeting. Ms. Wilson said she would prepare a report for Dr. Ivy and prepare for the next meeting with the next parent concern as listed.

The next day was Grandpa Marv's turn to pick Skye up from school. "Hi, Grandpa, Skye said as she got into his car. "Did you know you are very popular?" she grinned as she kissed him on his cheek. All my friends were talking about you during our talk break today." Grandpa Marv snapped, "That's because I'm cool!"

"No, Grandpa. I'm serious," she said. She went on to explain that most of her friends' parents were at that meeting last night and some of their children in the Special Education classes play basketball with my other classmates. Their parents told their children that you stood up for them." Feeling proud of himself, Grandpa Marv said, "Really?" What else did they say?"

"They said that you said they might not belong in those classes, and that some of them are in the class because they act up in their regular classes, or because the teachers don't understand them. Their parents said that you talked about ways to help them while they are in the program." Remembering a specific conversation, Skye said, "Oh yeah, they said that you said that the tests that they use isn't a good test to see who really belongs in the Special Education class. All of them said that they were really glad you were once a guidance counselor because you know exactly what needs to be done to make sure that they are in classes they belong in. Some of their parents didn't know why their kids were placed in the program because they didn't feel the testers or teachers gave them reasons they could understand. I guess what they really liked the most is that you care about them, and that you think they are smart."

"When people think others care about them, they will act and do better in their classes," said Grandpa. "I think everyone in a certain grade should be in regular classes unless they have a very special problem," said Skye. Responding to Grandpa Marv's question, Skye said, "I think that because we had group learning in Ms. Smith's class. She told us that when you work in a group, everybody gets smarter. She said no one knows everything, but everybody knows something. She said that is why lawyers and doctors work in groups. Ms. Smith said a lawyer or doctor usually checks with other lawyers or doctors about problems, because they know they might not know everything. She showed us how we get smarter when we have to figure out a way, to, explain something to someone so they understand. Ms. Smith said the person who didn't understand something becomes smart too, because they learned from the person sharing information," added Skye.

Thinking back to his own education, "I agree with you Skye. That's how Grandma Mary and I learned way back in the day. We learned that things don't have to stay the same, but if they do change, it should be for the better. I want to make sure that children at Whitney Magnet Public are treated fairly and receive a fair education."

"Grandpa, we didn't go anywhere! This is the first time we just sat at the curb in the car to talk," Skye said laughing. "It's your fault," Grandpa Marv replied. "Your friends' comments made me feel so good that I forgot to drive."

"Let's go for ice cream and go for a walk near the parlor until it is time to take you home," suggested Grandpa Marv as he pulled away from the school.

Story 16 ██████████████

Where justice is denied, where poverty is enforced, where ignorance prevails, and where any one class is made to feel that society is an organized conspiracy to oppress, rob and degrade them, neither person nor property will be safe. Frederick Douglas

Incarceration: Love Locked In

As an avid reader, Grandma Mary spends a lot of time in the library. Today, she is picking up books she has on hold at the Brooklyn Public Library. While there, she decides to borrow a few free DVDs for movie night with Grandpa Marv and Skye. Grandma Mary wonders how many people know all the wonderful offerings that the public libraries provide. She wonders how many people take advantage of the free access to computers, or that they can rent community rooms for birthday parties or organization meetings. The library even offers free private study spaces and even access to copy machines. Recently, several of the New York libraries launched their Read Down Your Fines programs. The program allows any NYPL card holders to waive overdue fines from his or her account at any library branch. The borrowers lose $1 of fines for each 15 minutes they read a book, magazine, newspaper, database, ebook, website, or even audiobook. Some people thought it was a crazy idea, because they figured that the library would never get items returned, but in fact, the opposite happened. The library has reported more people not only returning overdue books, but people are spending more time reading. Grandma Mary smiles as she glances over at the many latchkey children in the *Kid's Corner*. The library often sponsors activities for kids who are often left alone after school, so they have a safe space to interact with other children, get help with their homework, or just hang out to read. The award-winning library also has great summer programs, that include free meals for kids, and monthly book sales where you get to buy a whole bag of books for five dollars or less. As Grandma Mary checks out her books and DVDs, she talks to several of the librarians she recognizes from her frequent visits. She stops at the front desk to grab the monthly library calendar of events before leaving to pick Skye up from school.

"Hi, Grandma Mary," Skye said as Grandma Mary grabbed the library items from the passenger seat to put behind Skye's seat. She pulled up to the curb right on time. "What's up?" said Grandma Mary. Looking surprised at Grandma's energetic inquiry, Skye asks, "You don't want to know what I did in school today?" Telling Grandma Mary and Grandpa Marv is a regular afternoon routine for Skye. She always mentally reviews her day before the dismissal bell rings, so she has her discussion topic all ready when she gets into the car. Grandma chuckles as she smiles at Skye. "Of course, I do. I just decided to ask you the same question, but only using fewer words," she said with a smile. Skye told Grandma Mary that she didn't like talking about the day's activities unless something really interesting happened, but now she enjoys telling her about what she does every day." "I was hoping you'd feel that way," said Grandma Mary." All ready to share her story of the day, Skye began, "Well, today something sad happened. The kids were making fun of a boy named Jay because some of them found out he was in a picture on the front page of the newspaper. They said he was hugging his uncle, Samuel, who was just released from prison, on the courthouse steps."

"Yes, I saw that picture this morning Love," remembered Grandma Mary. She told Skye, "Your classmates must not have known that Jay's uncle served sixteen years, for a crime that he didn't commit."

"I wonder why Jay didn't just tell everybody that," said Skye. Skye went on to tell Grandma Mary that none of the students knew that Jay's uncle was even in prison. Skye said she felt bad for Jay when the other students were calling him a criminal, and said that prison is where he will end up, too. Not only was Grandma Mary surprised at how the kids behaved, but she was upset that Jay was subjected to this kind of treatment. "Did the teacher hear?" she asked. Skye explained to Grandma Mary that the bullying took place during recess when there weren't any teachers around. "But Grandma, I don't understand why the playground attendants watching us didn't make the kids stop. They acted like it was no big deal." Skye said, "One lady told the boys to stop, but I think she should have told them why. She knew what they were doing was wrong. After all, it wasn't like telling someone to stop hitting someone on the playground." Impressed with Skye's insight, Grandma Mary agreed with her.

As they pulled in the garage and then entering the house, Grandma Mary suggested they continue their conversation after they ate their snack. She reminded Skye that it isn't a good idea to talk about something stressful when you're eating. "Your tummy has a hard time digesting food when you are stressed," she explained. After changing out of her school clothes, Skye sat at the table to eat the large bunch of sweet red grapes and unsweetened lemon tea Grandma Mary prepared for her. While Skye was eating, Grandma Mary went to find the paper with the picture they were discussing on their way home. A few minutes later Grandma Mary joined Skye at the table with the newspaper in hand. Once they were done with their snack, she held the paper so that both she and Skye could see the picture of Jay and his uncle hugging. The picture almost took up the entire front page and they had smiles from ear to ear.
"Wow! They look so happy," said Skye. Suddenly Skye was even more upset with the day's events. "Grandma, those kids ruined Jay's happy feelings." Nodding, Grandma responded, "Yes. They did."

The *Wisdom Warrior* went on to explain to Skye that many people in prison were black, or people of color, but not all of them were guilty of the crimes they have been accused of committing. Grandma Mary read Skye most of the facts from the article about Jay's uncle. The article stated that the judge threw Samuel's murder conviction out because the evidence showed he wasn't even at the scene of the crime. Key witnesses admitted that they lied after he was in prison, but the other courts rejected Samuel's request for his case to be reexamined. After years of denied appeals and public protests, a judge agreed to review the case, only to find that Samuel was innocent. "Persistence was the key to Samuel's release Skye." "Persistence of his attorneys, the persistence on the part of the protestors, and Samuel's persistence to NEVER lose hope," Grandma Mary told Skye. Grandma Mary read other general facts about black imprisonment. The article stated that prisons are overwhelmingly filled with black and brown people, whose only crime is not having enough money for good lawyers to defend them from false accusations, or even of the minor crimes that other people serve far less time for committing.

Skye passionately stared at the picture of Jay's hugging and smiling with his Uncle Samuel.
"Grandma, I don't understand. None of this is fair. First, Samuel didn't do anything wrong. He spent all of my years of being alive and more in prison. And then Jay is made fun of because he is proud that his innocent uncle is set free. Grandma Mary, I feel so bad. I thought the courts are supposed to be fair to all people?" "Skye, let me try to explain this to you so you understand all the problems that lead up to this happening in the first place."

Desperately wanting to ease Skye's sadness, the **Wisdom Warrior** said, "Unfortunately, this form of discrimination has been around for a very long time, no matter where people traveled." She explained that far too often, people in power didn't believe they should treat people, who weren't like them, fairly. These people often do whatever it takes for them to be in charge, even if it means enslaving other human beings, destroying entire ethnic groups, and even imprisonment. When we think of prison, we think about a building like the one Jay's Uncle Samuel was in. However, prison can be in a person's mind. Just think about when people as a whole, or even an individual person, thinks less of himself/herself, simply because of the color of their skin or the texture of their hair. The only way people can be free, whether from a building or their mind, they must remain persistent, and keep pushing for what they know is right in their heart.

Wiping her tears away, Skye asked, "Grandma Mary, what can we do to help?"

"All your questions just gave me a great idea," said Grandma Mary,

"Really, Grandma Mary?" asked Skye.

"Really," Grandma Mary said with a big smile. "I am going to call Dr. Ivy to request a meeting for you and I to discuss everything you shared about Jay and his Uncle Samuel, as well as the kid's bullying Jay. I want you to tell your principal everything you told me so that he can speak to the adults who should have done more to help Jay. Then I'd like to discuss ways for the PTA to help raise money for Samuel to pay rent and other necessities, since it may take him some time to get a job," Grandma Mary told Skye. As she thought of other things they could do to help,

Grandma said, "Maybe Dr. Ivy will agree to have Jay's Uncle Samuel come speak to the students about being strong and persistent when bad things happen to them. Hopefully, Samuel will tell students that children shouldn't be blamed for the actions of adults, whether the adult is guilty or innocent." Grandma Mary thought as she watched Skye continue drying her eyes, "It is very sad that Jay had to suffer even though his uncle was innocent. Maybe, Samuel can even convince the students in Special Education classes not to give up, even though their education isn't the same as the other students. Success can be the best revenge. It means not giving someone permission to tell you who you are by proving them wrong."

Feeling much better, Skye thanked Grandma Mary for helping her understand what happened with Jay's uncle. "I know it is time to go home now. But I can't wait to tell the principal about Jay so he can feel better, "said Skye, as she picked up her back pack. "

Once they arrived at Skye's home, Grandma told her, "I will call Dr. Ivy first thing in the morning." "Okay. Bye, Grandma Mary! See you tomorrow," said Skye as she departed from the car.

Story 17

I prefer to be true to myself, even at the hazard of incurring the ridicule of others, rather than to be false, and to incur my own abhorrence. Frederick Douglass

Ancestors:
Rise and Shine

It is the first day of African American History month, and to Skye's surprise, Whitney Magnet Public students will have *two* assemblies instead of the usual monthly assembly in years prior. Ms. Smith announced that the first assembly will be with a surprise speaker, while the second assembly will be a student play at the end of the month. Skye remembers that past principals would leave it up to teachers to decide how the kids would celebrate. Most of the time there were just posters put up; the same ones every year. Other classes would do reports and special projects. This year, Dr. Ivy has told the teachers that they all had to do a project with their students, in addition to classroom summary posters of African American people the children select. Dr. Ivy wanted to make sure that all Whitney Magnet Public students felt valued by celebrating all cultures. Because African American children made up the largest population of the school, he especially wanted to make them feel special, and for the other students to see them just as valuable as any other student. He also adjusted the daily announcements for the entire month of February. There will be the usual daily announcements and the deep breathing exercise before the start of class, but there will also be an interesting African American History fact or quote.

Members of the PTA and Grandma Mary, met with Dr. Ivy the previous September to request a speaker for the first day of African American History month. They discussed how they thought a true celebration of the month would help boost the morale of the students, so Dr. Ivy agreed thinking it was a great idea. The students are typically excited on assembly days. Since Dr. Ivy's arrival, there seems to be more variety and interest by both the students and the parents. The teachers and Dr. Ivy noticed that today all of the African American students were feeling special in a way that they never had before, because *ALL* classes were celebrating African American history as part of American History.

Once the last class was seated in the auditorium, Dr. Ivy approached the podium and announced the speaker. He told the audience they were going to love today's speaker. Skye whispered to her friend Donte, sitting next to her, that she doubted she'd like the speaker more than Dr. Luke. A few minutes later, Dr. Ivy said, "Let's all welcome Dr. Luke to the stage." The students all screamed with excitement, high fived, fist bumped, and clapped as he energetically appeared from behind the curtain. "Welcome, my family," he said. As he began his speech, he reminded the audience, "We are all one human family, made up

131

of all cultures in this auditorium. Your history *is* American history because you all are part of *this* country." He went on to say, "Maybe one day, the history of all cultures living in America, will be in the history books that you study from. For now, we will use the calendar to remind us of special cultural moments, to celebrate and learn about each other's cultures. Learning creates understanding, and understanding creates respect for our individual uniqueness; so that we can live peacefully among one another."

As Dr. Luke approached the highlight of his presentation, he thanked Dr. Ivy and the PTA for the honor of speaking to this, "spectacular crowd of young people." Then he turned back to his audience and told them, "No students, I am not going to stand up here and just talk to you today. So, I want you to listen very carefully to my questions, because you and I will have a *conversation* during this entire assembly." Making eye contact with everyone in the audience, he asked, "Is that okay with you?" With a thunderous, "Yes," the children yelled in agreement. First, Dr. Luke took a moment to honor and thank Carter G. Woodson for creating African American History month, as to share the accomplishment of many forgotten Americans. Dr. Luke explained that the month was set aside to allow all cultures an opportunity to learn facts about people of African descent not recognized in the history books for their contributions in making America great.

As Dr. Luke began, he explained that he would first read from his list of questions to the children, then circle back to the first to answer them one-by-one.

Dr. Luke intentionally did this to allow the children some time to think about their answers.

"So here goes," he said, as he read the first question from his list of questions. 1.How many of you believe everything you think? 2. How many of you believe the things that kids who don't like you say about you? 3. Why do people like to be in charge? 4. If I want you to feel bad about yourself, what is something that I might say to you? 5. If I'm in charge of writing a book and I don't like you, do you think I will include you in the book? 6. If I don't like you, would I tell the truth about you if someone forced me to include you? 7. Is it normal for people to resist something bad? 8. Will those who resist always win? 9. How many of you know where mankind began?

Dr. Luke knew not everyone would remember all of the questions, but he also knew each child would mentally choose one or more questions to think about, and prepare an answer for them. Once he finished reading the questions, he said, "Now raise your hand if you want to answer the question as I repeat it."

One student, John, quickly raised his hand once the first question was read. He answered, "No, I don't believe everything I think because I might think that somebody doesn't like me, only because they didn't speak to me. Someone may not talk to me because they were either having a bad day, or that they didn't see me." Then Dr. Luke asked the students, "How many of you agree?" Almost every hand went up. Suzy replied to the second question by telling the students that of course, she doesn't believe the things kids who don't like her say, because they only want me to feel bad. She added, "Why would they say something nice if they don't like me?" Again, almost everyone agreed. Samantha said people love to be in charge because they can make all the decisions that only benefit them. Again, all hands went up in agreement. Skye said if she wanted someone to feel bad about themselves, she would say something mean and untrue to and about them, and again, almost every hand shot up. Robert said there was no way he would include people he didn't like in his book, "even if the people belonged in the book."

"No way," everyone shouted when Dr. Luke asked if they would include a person they disliked. Sue said with some reluctance, "No, I wouldn't tell the truth about someone I didn't like, because I would want people to not like them too. I would probably tell a big lie and convince people I was telling the truth."

"Yes, it is normal to resist something bad," answered Shirley. All hands shot up to Dr. Luke's inquiry. With a little hesitation, Melissa said, "No, you can't always win when you resist something. If someone has a weapon, or they're bigger than you, then you won't try to resist anymore, and then you can't win." Up went several hands again. Skye's hand was the only hand to go up when Dr. Luke asked about mankind. She proudly announced, "Mankind began in Africa," Once all of the questions had been asked and answered, Dr. Luke said, "You students are very clever. Your outstanding reasoning and responses are all connected to my presentation for today.

He began with the last question first, "Mankind did begin in Africa." Everyone except Skye looked shocked. Dr. Luke went on to explain that in fact, all human beings came from Africa, and then traveled to all parts of the world. In order to adapt to various climates, people evolved with certain facial features, hair textures, and skin tones in response to their environment. In general, Africans have coarse hair, wider noses, and darker skin tones as protection in the warmer climate, while Europeans developed pale skin, long hair, and narrower noses so their bodies could absorb more of the sun and inhale colder climates. There are no superior cultures; each culture differs as a result of evolution, and the need to survive in our natural environments.

"We are all equally a part of the human race," said Dr. Luke. He pointed to African and European people on the screen, and explained that it's when one race decided they were superior to other races; that genocide and slavery began. He explained that slaves who were unknowingly brought to America over 400 years ago, resisted in every way they could on their journey. They were always fighting for freedom, but some textbooks would have you believe otherwise. So, the writers of the textbooks either left African American facts out of their books, or told lies to make others not like them.

"Many of you feel embarrassed when the word slave comes up, because you know nothing about them." Dr. Luke reminded his audience that they had just said they would tell lies about someone they didn't like. "The bottom line is," explained Dr. Luke, "Slaves did nothing wrong. It is the masters who purchased another human being as property that should feel embarrassed for the unspeakable torture they forced on Africans and African American slaves." If most of the slaves didn't resist, African

Americans would not be here today. So, you should be proud of what your ancestors accomplished for you to have the life you have today."

As Dr. Luke ended his presentation, he told his audience, "Students, I want you to leave here today believing in the truth, and the desire to always seek the truth. Don't let others force you to believe what you haven't checked out for yourself. We must live as one family, made up of all the people who live in our world if we want to have peace. Do your part to make peace by treating each other as equals." As he bid them a farewell, he yelled, "I love all of you."

Once the students were dismissed, Skye ran out of the building to meet Grandpa Marv. To his surprise, Skye buckles herself in, looked up at him, and started crying. "What's wrong, Brown Sugar?" Grandpa asked with great concern. Then Skye, with a bright eyed smile, said, "Don't worry grandpa, I'm crying happy tears." With much relief, Grandpa Marv responded, "I'm happy to hear that. You have never cried happy tears in all the times that I picked you up from school." Skye chuckles as she wiped her tears, "I know Grandpa, but I'm so happy because this was the most special day ever." As Grandpa Marv drove away from the school, Skye began sharing with him the details about Dr. Luke's return as a guest speaker. She explained that she loved his presentation because all of the students got to experience a *Wisdom Warrior* event, like those she shares with Grandpa Marv and Grandma Mary.

"Even though you and Grandma Mary have talks with me all the time about why black people are treated so differently, I don't think a lot of the kids, especially the white kids, ever heard the information that Dr. Luke talked about today," Skye explained. With more tears of joy, Skye told him that all the black students were so happy that Dr. Luke talked about their history in such a special way. "Grandpa, everybody liked Dr. Luke!" This is my very favorite year at Whitney Magnet."

Skye was so excited about sharing today's events with Grandpa Marv, that she hadn't noticed they weren't driving to his house, and she hadn't even touched her juice box and fruit cup he had prepared for her snack. Once Grandpa Marv pulled into the hardware store parking lot, he told Skye they would pick up a few things and then he would take her home. Grandpa Marv noticed Skye seemed to have an extra stride in her step today. She walked with added pride because she was with a *Wisdom Warrior*, someone who reaffirmed her value as a special human being, and that affirmation was confirmed and shared with other children just like her by Dr. Luke, another *Wisdom Warrior*.

Once she was home, Skye said, "Bye, grandpa. I love you."

"I love you, too," he waved.

Story 18

> *Remember that sometimes not getting what you want is a wonderful stroke of luck.*
> Dalai Lama

Health:
Food Factors

Most kids don't think much about health. After all, they're kids. They think they can eat anything they like, and what they *really* like is fast foods, sweets, and other foods that bring a smile to their faces. It's a fact, that the brighter the colors of the drinks, the better they taste. Most kids only care about what foods look and taste like. So, Skye's class was not happy about having to attend a school assembly where the speaker is going to talk about health and food. After all, they are young, so whatever they eat, will not hurt them like it will adults. Besides, Skye has the best of both worlds, she has Grandpa Marv who lets her enjoy foods that some might consider unhealthy from his secret stash, while Grandma Mary tries to balance things out with the healthy snacks.

Ms. Smith, Skye's teacher this year, has also told the students that the speaker will talk about the health risks associated around cellphones and the Internet. Skye wondered, "What could the Internet possibly have to do with health?" With a confused look on her face, she noticed her classmates were thinking the same thing. "You don't eat the Internet", snarled Jameel as he whispered to his friend Tave. Ms. Smith wouldn't give the students any more clues about what the speaker was going to talk about, but she advised them that the assembly was very important and to listen carefully. Of course, she also reminded her class of the proper behavior during an assembly, and told them they needed to bring their notebooks with them.

To ensure the students were listening, Ms. Smith instructed them to write down at least five important facts about health, and another five important facts about the Internet. She told them that she would have three students share out loud from their lists every day, until all the facts were shared. When the students started to moan, Ms. Smith said, "Okay. Never mind, I will just test you on all the information from the speaker." Shocked by her new decision, Melissa asked, "Ms. Smith, can we vote on how we can show you that we were listening and know the information?" Ms. Smith smiled and agreed to let class vote. The students really liked Ms. Smith, especially when she allowed them to have some say in the way they learn different subjects. Once the vote was completed and the results tallied, seventeen of the students voted to orally share their facts, while three voted to take a test. Ms. Smith laughed and said," "I knew you would see it my way."

When it was time, the students quietly filed in and sat down in the auditorium, expecting to be bored. Ms. Taylor, the speaker, announced the name of the play the students would see about health and the Internet. Surprised that they weren't going to have to listen to a person talk to them for the next hour, the students shared smiles with each other and gave high-fives. The curtain lifted and there were so many people dressed like different types of foods and drinks. As the play began, the bad foods and drinks were making fun of the good foods, like the vegetables and fruits. At first, it seemed as though the bad foods were winning the word battle, but soon, the bad food and drink characters became very hyper, then they got super tired, and some even became ill. In fact, as the play continued, the bad food didn't want to do much, except sleep or play couch games. All throughout the play, the good food and vegetables maintained their energy level. No matter what was going on, they wanted to go out and play. The good food also remained focused in school, and didn't get sick. In the end, the good food and drinks had to take care of the bad food characters, and bring them back to health. The bad food and drinks were so grateful that they became friends with the good food and drinks. Having enjoyed the play so much, all of Ms. Smith's students forgot to write their facts down. Realizing her class was getting concerned about not completing their assignment, Ms. Smith whispered that they could write their facts down once they returned to class.

After a ten-minute intermission, Ms. Taylor announced the second presentation and the curtain rose again. The characters in this play were a variety of kids, about the same age as the Whitney Magnet

140

Public School students attending the assembly. Some of the kids were playing on their tablets, or phones, while ignoring everyone around them. When they walked around, they tripped on objects or even ran into each other. At one point, someone got seriously injured from falling into a fountain they didn't see because their head was down. No one could get their attention; because they were so into their games. In the school scene, the students couldn't even pay attention. They didn't find their teacher to be as entertaining as their games, and she didn't deliver the information as their computers did; much like a fast food experience. The worst two problems demonstrated were the constant moodiness, and health issues as a result of gaining weight from sitting too much, and from the lack of physical exercise. The other group of characters had kids without tech devices. They were excited about class discussions, loved communicating with each other, and even discussed with the teacher. They played different types of games together, and enjoyed being outdoors. All around, this group appeared to be very happy. Once the performance was over, the Whitney Magnet Public students cheered loudly for both plays.

When the students returned to class, Ms. Smith changed the assignment from writing down facts, to writing down what they learned from the plays. After time was up, Ms. Smith had three students share what they learned, beginning with Skye. Skye went to the front of the room and read what she had learned from the plays. She said that she learned that good food may not be as much fun to eat as bad food, but that the body likes good food because bad food can make kids very sick, moody, or too tired to do regular activities. Skye said she also liked when the play showed that eating sweets in small portions is okay, as long as most of the food we eat are fruits, vegetables, and other foods that don't have too many preservatives or fake chemical coloring that's not good for the body. Then Skye shared that she loved the group of characters that didn't spend a ton of time on the Internet. She said the Internet group was lonely, got hurt, and didn't do anything else to have fun. Skye loved how much fun the kids who didn't have the Internet, enjoyed participating in school discussions, and other fun activities.

"Nice job, Skye," beamed Ms. Smith. After the other two students shared what they learned, it was time to go home. The teacher gave them pamphlets on healthy foods and Internet use, to take home for their parents.

"Hi, Grandma Mary," Skye said as she jumped in her 4 Runner. Before Grandma Mary had a chance to ask about Skye's day, Skye began telling her, "We saw two funny plays during assembly today about healthy foods and unhealthy foods. Then there was a second play about the unhealthy things related to the Internet." As Skye shares what she learned and presented in front of her class, Grandma Mary couldn't help but be very impressed with Skye. Today, Grandma Mary made fruit smoothies with a little honey, mango, pineapple, and coconut for their healthy snack. While placing a spoonful of the smoothie in her mouth,

Skye was still thinking about the plays and remembered to give Grandma Mary the pamphlet from her backpack. As they ate their snack at the table, Grandma Mary looked at the pamphlet and went over the contents with Skye.

As Grandma Mary read through the pamphlet, Skye noticed the cover and asked, "Why are there mostly black people on the pamphlet cover Grandma, Mary? Don't white people need to eat just as healthy as black people? Hey, there are mostly black people with phones and video games? Everybody plays video games!" Grandma Mary smiled at Skye's observations and said, "The answers are all here in the pamphlet." "Everyone needs to eat healthy food, regardless of their race. However, not everyone has access to healthy food and even when it is available, it's often too expensive. Do you remember when grandma told you about the corner stores in the neighborhood she grew up in?" Skye nods her head up and down in agreement. Then Grandma Mary says, "And do you remember how I told you there were some nights my siblings and I went to bed hungry? Again, Skye agrees. Grandma explained to Skye that black people tend to make up the largest percentage of low-income consumers, so when they have money for food, they have to consider how much food they can buy, as opposed to how good the food is for them. Like the family I grew up in, a big bag of sugary cereal not only costs less than a box of healthy granola cereal, but it also feeds more mouths for a longer period of time. The cereal might not be healthy, but it stops hunger pains for a little while. She continues, "Many black people don't get to eat healthy for a lot of reasons, but a majority of them just can't afford to eat better." To help Skye understand the disparity between low income families and those who can afford healthy foods, Grandma Mary talked about some of her classmates.

"Skye you know some of your classmates' families can't afford healthy foods, so they get free breakfast and lunch to be sure they have a balance of both." "Like when you're with me and Grandpa Marv." She explained. Grandma Mary added, "Another reason that blacks eat less healthy is not listed in this pamphlet. Our ancestors were forced to eat bad food during slavery. The slaves were only given scraps from their owners' main meals, and they had to scrounge up what they could find in the vegetable gardens, like greens. Lard and other detrimental seasonings were used to help make these unhealthy foods taste better. Unfortunately, this way of eating has been passed down from generation to generation. African Americans are at the top of the list of all major diseases, like diabetes and high blood pressure. These unhealthy eating habits begin as children, and continue into adulthood.

"People don't realize that the way we eat as children, sets us up for future adult disease."

"Wow, Grandma Mary! What about the Internet? Black and white kids love the Internet." "This is very true, Skye," said Grandma Mary. She goes on to explain that statistics show black children spend more time alone with the Internet than their white counterparts, as result of their parents working more or longer hours. White parents are shown to monitor the amount of time their kids are on the Internet more than black parents. In fact, it has been proven that black kids spend three times more hours a day on the Internet, than white children.

"Skye, can you imagine how many important things could be accomplished in those extra three hours?"

Grandma asked. "Yes, I can," Skye replied. Skye told Grandma Mary that the kids could be doing homework, reading a book, meeting with friends, exercising, or so many other things they need to do. "Absolutely," said Grandma Mary.

"Oh, my goodness, look at how much time we've spent talking!" said Grandma Mary as she grabbed her sweater and Skye in tow., they raced out of the house to the car to get Skye home. Once they were in the car, they sang songs together until they reached Skye's home. "Take care," Grandma Mary said as she hugged Skye. "Love you," said Skye. "Love you, too," responded Grandma Mary.

Story 19

> *We need more light about each other. Light creates understanding, understanding creates love, love creates patience, and patience creates unity.* Malcolm X

Mental Illness: Minds Matter

A few weeks ago, letters were sent home to all parents and guardians of students attending Whitney Magnet Public. The letter requested topics of discussion for the school year. The Black Parent Association met a few months prior, to discuss issues they felt were especially important in regards to their students. The parents listed their concerns in the order of personal importance. Once most of the association forms had been returned, another letter was sent out the following week announcing that child abuse, mental illness, and substance abuse were voted as the top three topics of concerns among the association parents.

The general assembly offered different suggestions. The association letter included African American speakers specializing in these three specific areas, with additional dates for the first three Black Parent Association meetings.

One of Skye's friends, Denise, in another class, left the opened follow-up letter of speaker topics on her desk. She noticed there were two different calendars, one for general assemblies and another for the Black Parents Association. Then Skye overheard Denise's teacher, who was white, whispering about the letter to a black teacher in the hallway. She said she didn't understand why the black parents had segregated their meetings. "Isn't that what the PTA is for?" she asked the other teacher. She continued, "Black parents would charge the school district with discrimination if we had a white parent meeting." Her friend, Ms. Washington, patiently explained to Ms. Arnold that anyone is invited to attend the meetings requested by the Black Parent Association. She stated that the meeting is not designed to exclude anyone, but rather discuss issues and problems unique to their community and culture. Ms. Washington pointed out that the general assemblies were often just that, general. However, she showed Ms. Arnold that the issues being discussed at the association meetings were about specific issues often shunned in the black community, and once identified, parents lack the knowledge and resources to access to unique needs of their families. Ms. Arnold appeared to be nodding her head at the enlightening explanation. The bell rang, and both teachers disappeared into their nearby classrooms. The day had arrived for the workshop on mental illness. Ms. Robinson was thrilled that the weather was cooperating, because that would help ensure a good parent turnout. It was warm, but misty. When the clock struck 7:00 P.M., the room was almost completely filled with parents. As usual, parents mingled and chatted with friends before the meeting began promptly at 7:30 P.M. Ms. Robinson noticed

147

that the atmosphere wasn't as joyful as it usually is before meetings, and when the meeting began she scanned the faces of all the attendees, and their faces seem to say that they hoped this meeting wouldn't be a waste of their time. She winked at Grandma Mary when their eyes met.

Ms. Robinson began Ms. Sterling's introduction by reading credentials, work history, and contributions in the field of mental health. Ms. Sterling thanked Ms. Robinson and then she said with a very solemn voice, "I'm not a mind reader, but I can guess what most of you are thinking right now." She continued,
"I believe most of you are here because you have heard about so many tragedies in the news surrounding mental illness. But you're all curious to learn what these issues have to do with your young children. Am I correct?" Murmuring amongst one other, the adults nodded in agreement. Ms. Robinson could sense the group had started to relax because Ms. Sterling's voice was soothing, yet authoritative. The mental health expert explained, "My brief story will soon answer your question. On top of that, the story I am about to tell you is true." She stared into the audience and quietly began, "The other day an eight- year old African American girl tried to commit suicide. Her young single mother had three children, and the landlord of the only housing she could afford blatantly told the mother, in front of her children, that she could only have two children in the apartment. So, the youngest child, Cheryl, who was already feeling like a burden, had to pretend she was a visitor so the mother wouldn't get evicted. Cheryl thought that since she was the youngest of the children, not really capable of contributing anything, thought she should kill herself, so her mother would no longer

have to worry about supporting three children, while pretending one was not her child." Everyone gasped in disbelief. After a short pause, Ms. Sterling said, "I am so happy to tell you that Cheryl did not succeed, and is getting the help she so desperately needs. But tragically, there have been so many more African American kids like Cheryl who have succeeded." Ms. Sterling went on to explain that mental health is a very serious problem for African American adults and children. She explained, "As an African American psychologist, I say this because many of you might not agree. Please remember that just because we don't think something is a problem, doesn't mean that it isn't. Avoiding a problem causes more stress, but facing reality causes less stress in the long run."

As Ms. Sterling continued her speech, she reminded the attending parents that children often experience the stress of problems just like their parents. While not in the same way, she explains they face discrimination in their classroom, on the playground, and even in simple conversation. She states that kids know when a teacher, or other professionals, are treating them unfairly because of how they look, or even how they dress differently. It's just as difficult for children to deal with these kinds of problems, as adults. However, kids don't think like adults. They cope the best way they know how. Some cope by acting out, others become depressed, others by shutting down in school and refusing to participate or complete assignments. She urges, "As parents you must be attentive to your child's moods. You know your child best, but sometimes what is best for your child is your help, combined with that of a professional." Giving an example, she says, "When

you're on a plane, the flight attendant instructs you to put your oxygen mask on first, and then to proceed to help your child. They understand you can't help your children if you can't function, due to the lack of your own oxygen. Well, the same holds true with mental illness." She explains that African Americans tend to be a very religious community. So, she says she likes to think of prayer as the "oxygen mask" we should wear first. Then she says, once the prayer oxygen mask is on, you or your child might require a professional's help to avoid any further complications." Ms. Sterling lets out a serious chuckle and says, "We are not superhuman. No one looks down on anyone who seeks medical help for any part of their body that is injured, except when the brain is physically injured. Think about how ridiculous that sounds. The brain is more precious to the body than any other body part, because it signals actions to all of the other body parts." Again, she pauses to allow the audience a moment to consider what she has said, "The brain is very complex, so it doesn't make sense to think that fixing particular brain problems due to severe stress, serious injury, or trauma would be simple. Experts overwhelmingly agree that mental problems kill, because mental stress from trauma causes several other diseases." With disappointment in her voice, she says,
"Unfortunately, African Americans top the list of most serious and deadly of these diseases."

Ms. Sterling winds her speech down by explaining,
"We have the trauma of our ancestors running through our veins. Seeking help is a sign of strength, not weakness. The everyday stress of systemic racism and oppression can cause severe mental stresses. As one who grew up in the same community, I

150

understand your mistrust with the medical profession due to poor and biased medical treatment. Some of you may know about the deceptive and fatal experiments that were once forced on African Americans, without our permission. There are also problems with doctors failing to arrive at the right diagnosis for so many African Americans, because they refuse to recognize and explore our unique physical make up. African American therapists are scarce, and African Americans lead in the statistics of those without health insurance. However, the worst problem is not believing that there is a problem. Ms. Sterling encourages the listeners to be inspired by all the famous African American celebrities like Jay Z, Tyler Perry, Kid Cudi, and more who see therapists and highly recommend therapy for the African American community. The National Alliance on Mental Illness, and government agencies, will answer questions and get you or your loved one help." She ended her talk by answering questions and passing out pamphlets about recognizing signs of mental illness in adults and children. In all, the workshop was a great success.

The next day, Grandpa Marv is outside waiting to pick up Skye. As he watches her emerge through the school door, he feels so grateful that Skye has her parents, along with him and Grandma Mary, to help soften the blow of life's stress and problems that she might need assistance with to overcome. "What are you thinking about Grandpa Marv?" asks Skye as she grabs his hand. He looks down with a smile and says, "I was thinking about you Love. I was just thinking about how much I love talking to you when you need to feel better about anything that's bothering you." "Yeah, Grandpa! You and Grandma Mary, as my

Wisdom Warriors, along with my parents, help me so much. I use your talks all the time to help me figure out how to solve my own problems more than I use too," says Skye as she climbs in the car and buckles up. "That's because you are getting older Skye," explains Grandpa Marv. "Yes, but I also think it is because of all the lessons you've shared with me, help me learn how to solve my own problems." As he pulls away in the car, he asks, "Like what Skye?" She mentally recounts, "Well, today on the playground, this white boy said that his father said that black people are always using the race card to explain anything that happens to them. At first it made me mad, and I was going to call him stupid for listening to his dad. But then I realized that he would still think his dad was right unless I spoke up. So, I told him that he and his father wouldn't know if that is true, since they aren't black. And then I told him that it didn't matter to me what he or his dad thought. Grandpa, he just looked at me with a puzzled stare. I think he was actually thinking about what I said," explained Skye. Proud of how she handled today's challenge, Skye said, "Grandpa Marv, I'm not going to lie and pretend that it doesn't make me sad to explain to white kids why my hair is the way it is, or why my skin is the color it is all the time. They say stuff that makes no sense, but how else will they learn if somebody who knows the truth, doesn't try to give them true information." Looking over in amazement, Grandpa Marv says, "I am so proud of you." Breaking the silence of the ride, Skye says, "Oh, I almost forgot to tell you, that we had a short assembly this morning. Some lady came to talk to all of us about mental illness." "Oh good. That was the topic of the meeting Grandma Mary and I went to last night, with your dad. Ms. Sterling wanted to make sure she shared the same information with the kids whose parents couldn't make it last night." Seeing how attentive Skye was, Grandpa Marv said, "Skye I want you to continue to look out for those kids who don't seem to have friends at school. Everybody isn't as lucky, as you, Brown Sugar." Feeling good about Grandpa Marv's compliment, she says, "I know I'm lucky Grandpa. I don't like being mean to anybody. Most of the kids who are mean, are mean because somebody has hurt them, or they are jealous of kids who don't have to suffer like them."

Realizing they were still parked Skye exclaims, "Grandpa, this is the second time we just sat in the car to talk." He laughed and told her, "I was so absorbed in what you were saying that I wanted to give you my undivided attention, not the road." After they finished talking, Grandpa Marv drove to his house. Once in the kitchen, Skye sat and ate her oatmeal raisin cookies and drank her almond milk alone. Grandpa Marv went to the yard to finish some weeding. She ran upstairs to change her clothes once she was done and headed outside to join her grandpa in the yard, until it was time to go home. Once they were back in the car, Skye started singing a song she and her classmates sang in choir today called, *Let There Be Peace on Earth and Let It Begin with Me.*" Before Skye knew it, she was already home, "Bye, Grandpa," she said as she stepped into the house. "Bye, Brown Sugar," Grandpa Marv said as he blew her a kiss from her steps.

Story 20

> *It is easier to build strong children than to repair broken men.* Frederick Douglass

Child Abuse: The Call to Safety

Althea Hughes stood at the front of the room during the Black Parent Association meeting. Ms. Sterling waited for the final few parents to take their seats before introducing Ms. Hughes as the speaker on the topic of child abuse. Ms. Sterling read Ms. Hughes impressive qualifications and parents applauded as Ms. Hughes approached the podium and thanked Ms. Sterling for introducing her.

Ms. Hughes began her talk by saying that the job of a parent is to always love, honor, and protect their children by teaching them, and listening to them. She went on to say that she was going to speak about three types of child abuse, beginning with sexual abuse. If children don't feel safe, they can't focus in school because they are focused on their trauma.   She cautioned the parents, "We have a very tragic crisis that has been going on far too long, and now it has gotten to the point where we must stop the bleeding." She said, "I'm sure all of you are familiar with the crisis in the Catholic Church where you would expect children to be safe and protected by clergy, but instead they are being abused on a massive scale." Ms. Hughes went on to explain that sadly, the church has not condemned the abusers as fiercely as it condemns church members for not following its teachings. She further explains that unfortunately, the Catholic Church is not alone in the abuse of children. Clergy from other denominations across the country have also been found guilty of such a crime. Ms. Hughes says, "I use the church as an example because most people believe that religious leaders can be trusted."

Using another example, Ms. Hughes states, "As African Americans, you are more familiar with the R. Kelly case." She continues, "While I am not going to talk about R. Kelly today, I mention him because it tends to catch the attention of the African American community. And since the publicity of his abuse is now out in the open, people in our communities have begun to seriously talk about the sexual abuse of children." Ms. Hughes explained that the abuse of African American children can be traced back to slavery. Children were abused in the same torturous and unspeakable manner adults were. Today, children are blamed by adults for not being able to stop the abuse, or being accused of asking for the abuse because of their actions or attire. With a very strong stern voice, she says, "Let me be crystal clear, children are *never* ever responsible for any adult behavior, period. Regardless of any behavior on the part of a child, it is never, ever their fault."

As Ms. Hughes continued her speech, recounting examples of stories where guilty offenders didn't fit the description of someone who would abuse a child. The first story was about a religious family, whose members appeared to be very loving and nurturing. Several members of the family babysat for working parents in their home for years. Unfortunately, none of the children told their parents about the abuse until they were adults. One of the abused children explained to her parents that their house seemed so happy, that she felt if she told anyone about the abuse, it wouldn't be that way anymore. As an adult, she shared she felt she could tell her parents, and she knew they would believe her, but she didn't want to sacrifice their happiness. Ms. Hughes cautioned the audience, "So I say to you now, don't assume everything is normal just because it appears to be so. The mother of that child had been abused herself, so she thought she would be able to spot abusers."

Then Ms. Hughes told parents that they must teach their children about "good and bad touching". "Don't assume children know the difference. Bad touching is any private area of a person's body." She warned the parents that most children are abused by someone they know, including other siblings. Ms. Hughes emphasized that anyone can be an abuser. In fact, she stated that the abuser of the children in the example she shared was a female. She abused both male and female children. She explained that parents shouldn't force children to show affection by kissing, hugging, or sitting on a person's lap. "Think about it," she said. "How would you like to be forced to kiss, hug, or sit on the lap of someone you don't want to?" She added, "If your child tells you they are being abused, then believe them!" Abusers are very clever people who have many ways to scare a child into not telling, so if your child seems uncomfortable around certain people, ask the child why they feel uncomfortable. Your child is far more precious than the family member you may be afraid of offending or protecting. She said this is also true of boyfriends, a spouse, or any other individual that you don't want to lose a relationship with, and many other special relationships. Ms. Hughes said that she is so very grateful to people like Oprah Winfrey, Tyler Perry, Maya Angelou, and other African American celebrities, for sharing the abuse they suffered as children. They are examples to children that they can still achieve their dreams by getting help from a professional.

Ms. Hughes moved to the next kind of abuse. "Now let's talk about physical abuse," she said. Grandma Mary looked around and was happy to see that the woman she saw slap her child, was there with her friend. "I know it can be very difficult to be a parent," said Ms. Hughes. "As parents, we are aware of the hardships they will face as black children in this country and we want to raise them to be tough enough to survive prejudice, but beating them is not the answer," she explains. I want all of you to read Dr. Patton's article written in *The New York Times* called "*Stop Beating Black Children*." In the article, Dr. Patton explains that slave owners taught us to beat our children. Our ancestors treated children very special. She tells us that spankings lead to beatings, and beatings often lead to the death of a child; which is highest in the African American culture. There were gasps of disbelief from the audience. Hughes told parents to search for support groups or books on discipline to help them develop safe and loving discipline techniques.

Lastly, Dr. Hughes explained that not listening to your children's concerns, calling them names, or saying inappropriate things to them out of frustration, is emotional abuse. Our job, as parents, is to help our children become their very best selves. Dr. Hughes pleads with the parents, "I know many of you are exhausted from trying to make ends meet, but you will have to be creative if you want a happy and content child." She suggested that parents have their children draw, or even write down questions about their feelings using journals or drawing pads. She explained that this is often a non-threatening way to share their thoughts and feelings to discuss when you can make time. She ends her speech with, "Always remember that you *chose* to be a parent."

It is Monday, and all of the Whitney Magnet Public students file into the auditorium for a health assembly. Ms. Hughes is introduced by Dr. Ivy, the principal. "Thank you, Dr. Ivy," Ms. Hughes says as she gives her young audience a warm smile and tells them how very special they are, and how much she loves helping children. "You are the sunshine of life," she says to them. Then she tells a few very silly jokes that have the children giggling and laughing. When she feels the kids are relaxed, she explains that lots of things in life are funny like her jokes, but there are also lots of serious things that need to be talked about. "So, I need all of you to give me your full attention, because I need to talk to you about a very serious topic." Ms. Hughes said people don't like to talk about bad things, but if we don't talk about these things then they will keep happening and never get fixed.

She stood taller, "So today, I want to talk to you about "good and bad touching", and how nothing bad that happens is *ever* a child's fault. *Ever*," she repeated in a booming voice. Ms. Hughes told the young audience everything she told the parents at the parent meeting. Most of the children were already prepared for her topic because several parents had already discussed it at home. However, she said some things that she didn't tell the parents. Ms. Hughes told the students that if anyone touched them in a bad way, they were encouraged to talk to the school counselor, if they were afraid to talk to a parent. She explained that the school counselor was there to help them with solving their problems.

She gave an assignment to all the teachers to give to all the students. She had copied a ***Dear Abby*** article out of the newspaper that was written by elementary school children, requesting advice to stop someone who was abusing them. Teachers were instructed to read the two problems to their classes, and the students had to give advice based on Ms. Hughes talk. Teachers of lower grade students were to record classroom responses on chart paper and the older grades were to complete their assignment on loose leaf paper. Ms. Hughes liked to use this activity because upper grade students would sometimes, disclose that the same thing was happening to them, as they offered advice to the writer. The lower grade students were often made to feel more comfortable sharing with their teacher if they were experiencing a similar problem. When the activity was completed, teachers were instructed to give the school counselor copies of any assignments that could be a red flag for kids indicating a problem. This way, the school counselor could get them help as soon as possible. Teachers were also encouraged to reteach the messages Ms. Hughes taught based on student responses.

"Hey Grandpa," said Skye. As she climbed into the car, she said, "we had a deep discussion in our health assembly."

"I know," said Grandpa. Looking at Grandpa Marv with a sly grin, Skye responds, "Oh, I get it. The same person that talked at your meeting, came to our school. Just like the last meeting." Smiling back, Grandpa Marv said, "That's true. But the message for adults is always different than the one for the children. So, tell me about it." Skye really didn't feel like talking about the topic, because it made her feel sad to think that kids are abused. Even though she liked the activity that they had to complete, she still felt sad for the kids. "Grandpa Marv, I just want to tell you about the activity we did." Noticing Skye's reluctance, Grandpa Marv said, "Okay. That's fine by me." Skye told him how she loved activities that made her think. She explained how she gave advice to a kid who wrote about his abuse problem. Skye's teacher, Ms. Smith brought an article from an advice column, and shared it with the class. Then, Skye explained how she shared with the class her advice to the kid. "What advice did you give him?" Grandpa Marv asked intrigued. Skye said she told the kid that he was very brave and very smart to write *Dear Abby*. She also told him that she really admired him because he figured out a way to get help. "Grandpa, he even said in his letter that he didn't blame himself," said Skye. Skye went on to tell Grandpa that her teacher, Ms. Smith, said most kids blame themselves. "So, I told him he is very special because he knew he didn't do anything wrong." Then Grandpa Marv said, beaming with pride, "I loved everything you said to him, counselor Skye." Skye laughed with Grandpa Marv and said, "Very funny, Grandpa!"

Skye got out of the car to go into Grandpa Marv's house. On the table was a small bowl of pineapples and a glass of water. Skye decided to practice the old school game of jacks that Grandma Mary taught her. She loves the game, but she will love it more when she can beat Grandma Mary. When it was time to go home, Skye had to borrow Grandma Mary's umbrella because it was raining so hard outside.

"See you later, alligator," Grandpa Marv said as she got out of the car. "After a while crocodile", she replied back. She left the umbrella in the car and was totally soaked when her mom opened the door. They waved and blew kisses to Grandpa Marv as he drove off.

Story 21 █████████

Substance Abuse: Warrior with a Future

Grandma Mary is thinking about tonight's Black Parent Association meeting as she does her daily chores. She is hoping that attendance will continue to be great. She knows how difficult it is to deal with the daily struggles of injustices living as a black person in America. So, attending such stressful meetings in the evening, is not the way to relax after a hard day's work. Grandma Mary feels that Dr. Ivy is the main reason why attendance at the Black Parents' Association meetings have increased to a full house, and there was only room to stand when people showed up late. Dr. Ivy sent a letter to African American parents at the beginning of the school year, telling them that he is completely invested in helping all students, but particularly African American students. He said his reason was because he had inherited a school where their needs were ignored. He also stated that because of that fact, his administration inherited widespread discipline problems, poor school performance, and school personnel, that came to the wrong conclusions as to why these issues affected so many African American children.

Madison told her mom, Grandma Mary, that Dr. Ivy sent another letter home recently thanking African American parents for full and standing room-only meetings, but he desired to reach even more parents. So, he announced additional incentives to increase attendance at all future meetings. Dr. Ivy assured parents that he could get rid of the academic achievement gap, because all cultures are equally capable of performing socially and academically at the highest levels, when major obstacles are eliminated. Then he reminded parents that he could not achieve promises without the support of all parents and guardians. Grandma Mary thinks the incentives of a $25 gift card, and the chance to win additional prizes by having winners' names entered in a raffle, will definitely assure overflowing attendance at all future meetings.

Parents have already witnessed so many of the positive changes that Dr. Ivy has instituted at Whitney Magnet Public. Their children are always telling them about how much they like Dr. Ivy and about changes he made to the announcements, assemblies, and school spirit as a whole. Parents are relieved that they don't have to listen to their children telling them how much they hate school like in past years.

White parents are just as happy with Dr. Ivy because their children are just as content as the black students.

Whitney Magnet Public School truly lives by the slogan: We Are Family. Grandma Mary put up the vacuum and decided she was done with her chores for the day. She would do some relaxing activities and errands, until tonight's meeting on African Americans and Substance Abuse.

The meeting began promptly at 7:30 P.M. Grandma Mary, Grandpa Marv, and Madison's dad, Melvin were there, but Madison, Skye's mom, stayed home with her. Dr. Ivy introduced Dr. Williams as his best friend, and a leading expert in the field of substance abuse, and its terrible effects on African Americans. Dr. Williams is medium built, and he looks as though he works out. "Thank you for the introduction best friend," he smiled. "These people in the audience are smart enough to know that maybe you must have exaggerated my accomplishments, since you are my best friend." The audience laughed at his joke, but also laughed because he had the personality of a comic.

Dr. Williams began his speech with "My dear brothers and sisters, the issue I am addressing tonight is a tough one, but know that I am here to inform solely, not to judge anyone," he explained. "I am here to give you as much information as I can to let you know that substance abuse is a real problem that is affecting and destroying the lives of so many of our people. Life is so very hard for us because of the daily struggles with injustice, and the fact that so many white people ignore the injustices that take a toll on

African American parents, and their children." He continued, "I am not going to throw numbers at you to tell you how much of a problem it is in our community. You already know how serious substance abuse is because you, or someone you are connected to, is negatively affected by substance abuse. My message to you is to *talk* about the issues that cause abuse, and to give you suggestions on how to cope in a positive manner. Let's start by realizing that kids begin substance abuse around the age of 12, which is why I have been asked to speak to you this evening. Some kids are experimenting, but so many more are using in a way to numb the pain of all types of emotional, sexual, physical abuse, and even violence. Some students use because of issues that deal with mental illness, like depression. Drugs are rampant in our communities. Those of us living in poverty, use various drugs to deal with the stress. Billboards advertising tobacco and alcohol are all over our community. This racist practice promotes the message that drinking and smoking creates happy feelings. Please know that any drug is just a temporary fix. And prolonged use will cause chronic medical issues, and far more serious issues where a doctor might not be able to save you."

"There are also people in the audience who are in danger of abuse because it runs in families." Dr. Williams completed his talk by telling parents to google government agencies that can help with assistance with their problem. The bottom line is that if they confront the realities in their lives by using productive coping skills, their happiness can increase tenfold, despite all the stressful injustices in their life.

He ended with "Thank you so much for your attention and questions," as he left the podium. The parents gave him a warm applause.

Grandpa Marv was at the curb ready to pick Skye up from school. "Don't tell me Grandpa, I already know that you know Dr. Williams came to speak to us today about substance abuse." Trying to act surprised, Grandpa Marv, said, "Really? Who is Dr. Williams?"

"You're not funny Grandpa," Skye said trying to hide her giggle. "Okay, I confess," said Grandpa Marv while laughing. Skye told Grandpa Marv that Dr. Williams was a very good speaker." He was pretty funny, kinda like Dr. Luke," she added. "Do you want to know what he talked about?" Skye asked.

"Of course," said Grandpa Marv, as they began their journey home. Skye began telling Grandpa how Dr. Williams shared about how some kids begin experimenting with drugs around 12 years old. She tells him that she wasn't surprised, since she has heard kids at her school talk about how they tried cigarettes, snuck alcohol, or even tried weed. Dr. Williams talked about how dangerous all of these drugs are, and the problems that they would create with frequent use, explained Skye. Dr. Williams told the students that some kids aren't just experimenting; some are using drugs to cover up horrible problems in their lives. He recommended that students and parents talk to their school counselor, like Grandpa Marv used to be, when they learn about these kids and their drug problem, so they can get help. Skye said he finished his talk by telling the kids all the ways they can experience being a much happier person by not using drugs, regardless of what obstacles they face.

166

"Dr. Williams suggested joining clubs like chess, debate, dance, acting, and singing. He said if none of those ideas interested them, then they could use their own idea to create a club that they think many other kids would want to join. He said when a person enjoys or excels in something, happy feelings invade their bodies with only good consequences to their health. Dr. Williams's final recommendation was for kids who are under serious stress., should consider sports that require immense energy like running, basketball, volleyball, bicycling, boxing and swimming, to help with angry feelings."

"How did your classmates respond to Dr. Williams' talk Skye," asked Grandpa Marv.

"Well, I think most of us were worried that he was going to preach to us, and as you know, we don't like to be preached at. But he didn't preach at all. He told us at the beginning of his talk that he was a kid once, and never liked to be preached to either. So, he must have read our minds." Skye explained that Dr. Williams said stories about people with problems and helpful solutions were what helped him learn about things that were not good for him. Dr. Williams told the students that he learned early on in life, not to judge people because in all honesty, we don't know their private and sometimes serious struggles, especially our peers and their parents. She told Grandpa Marv the students gave him a standing ovation at the end of his talk.

Grandpa Marv and Skye ate their fruit popsicles when they got to the house. As she enjoyed the coolness of the frozen flavor, she reached for Grandpa Marv's paper to search for *Dear Abby* problems written by kids her age. Ever since her teacher had Skye's class solve the problem of a child her age, she regularly looks for different problems that she might be able to help solve, just for fun. Sure enough, there was a letter written by a 10-year old boy about his mother doing drugs. Skye read the problem out loud and told Grandpa Marv what her advice would be based on some of Dr. Williams' advice. "Good job," said Grandpa Marv.

On the way home, Skye just watches nature and people from the car window, and Grandpa Marv listens to his favorite radio host, DL Hughley. Skye loves listening to the sound of Grandpa Marv laughing at the radio hosts jokes. As the car comes to a halt, Skye jumps out and says, "Bye, Grandpa." Skye had to say it several times because Grandpa Marv was really into what DL Hughley was talking about. He finally looks up with a smile and says,

"Oh! Bye, Skye. See you tomorrow."

Story 22 ███████

Family Reunion: We are Family

It is the second week of August, and Skye's family is having a family reunion from Friday through Sunday. Madison asked her father, Grandpa Marv, to organize the event because he had so much experience as a counselor. Madison's favorite event that her father would organize every year was a college bus tour to Historically Black Colleges through Washington D.C., Atlanta, and Florida. Madison, and several of her friends, went on her father's tour during her junior year of high school and had an amazing time. The trip was a contributing factor in Madison's decision to attend Clark University in Atlanta, Georgia. Each year, the students get a guided tour of each campus, with an opportunity to sit in on some of the classes. They also see a film about exciting organizations and college life on the campuses they were visiting.

There are also admission presentations explaining the steps to apply. Most presentations include facts about the college, and their importance as a Historically Black College. In most cases, these colleges came to be because at one point in history, black students were denied admission into white colleges, so they created their own. Students didn't have to worry about racism on these campuses. In fact, they are encouraged to celebrate their uniqueness and be themselves. While attending Clark, Madison loved the caring professors and the educational atmosphere created by so many people who loved and embraced the African American culture.

Skye couldn't wait to see the bus load of relatives arriving from Ft. Lauderdale, Florida. She has so many cousins that she only gets to see every year at the family reunions. Some of the relatives are from Chicago and Atlanta. There were tents set up in Madison's backyard for a fish fry, and one of Grandpa Marv's best friends is catering, so she will be serving several types of fish that Grandpa Marv and his friends caught in a freshwater lake not far from the house. There was macaroni and cheese, coleslaw, creamed corn, salad, and also cakes, peach cobbler, and ice cream for dessert. For fun, the relatives played lots of board games. Sky loves getting together with her relatives; she especially loved Uncle Charles' jokes. He has a loud funny laugh and told funny jokes that caused tears to run down so many relatives' faces. Some relatives even complained that their stomachs hurt from laughing so hard. The fish fry ended around 9:00 P.M. so the bus can leave to take the Florida relatives back to their hotel. Everyone else drives to the same hotel that was only a few miles away.

170

On Saturday, everyone has breakfast on their own and after breakfast, all relatives crowded on the bus, because today, they were to take a tour of the host family city and its attractions, because this is the first time the reunion is in New York. Grandpa Marv's friend, who is just as funny as Uncle Charles, leads the tour of attractions. When Uncle Charles and Sylvester got together on the bus, it felt as though they were performing a comedy show. Skye and her cousins were laughing just as hard at the adults because they were being silly. After the tour, everyone was on their own to go to the mall, rest at the hotel, or go to some attraction that Sylvester showed them. Later, everyone would meet at a banquet hall for a family banquet at 6:00 P.M.

The parking lot was filled with cars as people filed into the banquet center. Everyone looked so nice. The DJ unloaded his equipment to set up, while the adults found their seats. Skye's dad, Melvin, called everyone to order as the last table filled up. Melvin had everyone at each table to hold hands as he prayed to bless the food. Madison directed the tables to the buffet style tables with chicken, corn bread, mashed potatoes, salads, roast beef, steak, collard greens, deviled eggs and more. There was a gigantic cake with the words Carew Family Reunion. After dinner, Melvin announced the events for the evening. The first event would be a lighting of a candle for every individual that passed that year. Then Melvin, beamed at his mother in law, as he announced grandma's name. She came to the podium and said how happy she was to see so many relatives. She called Skye to the podium to join her. Grandma talked about how much she loved caring for Skye after school, and how much she cherished their conversations. Then she told the family how Skye was the motivation for inspiring adults at Whitney Magnet Public, because of her, African American History month was even more special because our history is American History, which was being taught in the way that it should've been. Grandma said she realizes that all the children in the family may not attend a school like Skye, and so she wanted to create something unique so that all African Americans could celebrate African American History themselves. She announced that her *Living the Mission for African American Youth* lessons were to celebrate every day of the month of February and, she reminded the family, that the lessons are also meant to celebrate every day of every year, because we are African American every day of every year. The family agreed with loud cheers. The cousins passed out the lessons and volunteer cousins took turns reading each lesson aloud. Grandma and the cousins received a standing ovation.

The rest of the evening was spent dancing to DJ Still Bill's popular music. The family met for Sunday brunch at the hotel on Sunday before leaving to go back home. Skye went home with her grandma, while her parents handled some business related to the very successful family reunion.

"Grandma," said Skye, "I was so shocked when you called me to the podium. I had no idea why you called me up there. I loved reading those lessons out loud. All the cousins came up to me to tell me how happy they were that you created something very special for them to celebrate their culture. Most of them said they never heard about many of the lessons you wrote. I told them about some of the answers you give me to problems that I have. And I told them about how you and my parents tell me to speak up, as to inform my peers of things that they may not know about our culture. Then I told them to have their parents speak up at school if they don't think they are being treated fairly. I told them how you speak up when we go to different places, like when we went to Marshalls when you weren't treated properly. Some of my cousins say that it isn't any use to speak up, because many people don't care, but I told them what you said about nothing will change if people don't try to fix things. I think they get what I am talking about because they looked at me as if they understood. The last thing that I told them was that giving up is never the answer! They called me Grandma Mary." "That's funny," said Grandma."

"Grandma, I wish we could have a family reunion every year."

"I agree," said Grandma."

"There is so much that the cousins could do with the lessons," said Skye."

"Like what?" said Grandma.

"They could write down their feelings that they have about the lessons in their journals, and they could even ask the librarian for books on more information about those certain lessons. They could share the lessons with their schools, or they could have a conversation about them, make rap songs, or they could make them into art."

"Those are great ideas," said Grandma."

"Grandma, the most important thing they can do is feel as good as I do about belonging to a phenomenal culture."

"Yes, we are phenomenal! I love you Skye Carew!"
"I love you too, Grandma." When they arrived at
Grandma's house Skye went upstairs to take a nap
until her mom came to pick her up.

The 28 ████████

Lessons

If you don't like something change it. If you can't change it, change your attitude. Maya Angelou

LIVING THE MISSION FOR AFRICAN AMERICAN YOUTH

1. We will celebrate African American beauty. African American beauty comes in a variety of shades, facial features, and hair textures.
2. We will honor our ancestors who sacrificed their lives so that we may be free, by refraining from using the N word that was used to inflict unspeakable torture and death to the minds, bodies, and spirits of all African Americans.
3. We will educate ourselves because education allows for so many career choices, as well as financial stability.
4. We will attend vigilantly to our health because African Americans lead the nation in almost every chronic and terminal illness.
5. We are our brothers' keeper. We will celebrate our successes, and help those less fortunate than us.

6. We will read more to learn the truth about ourselves, because through learning the truth, we refuse to accept others false information about our people.

7. We will discipline ourselves to make positive choices regarding video games and TV viewing, because negative media choices adversely affect our thoughts and our actions.

8. We will respect each other by using positive language to express ourselves. Positive language uplifts the spirit and negative language demeans the spirit.

9. We will celebrate our rich cultural history every day of every year, because we are African American every day of every year, and not just during African American History Month.

10. We will choose role models based on their integrity, and not strictly because of their financial accomplishments and celebrity status.

11. We will research the vast career options within the professional sports world where we are severely underrepresented, because a very minute number of African Americans are chosen to play professional sports.

12. We will respect our elders for the wealth of wisdom they provide, because their wisdom will guide us in our pursuit of positive physical, spiritual, and educational choices.

13. We will honor the memory of our past and present African American leaders by researching information about them through museum viewings, the Internet, and reading about them.

14. We will demonstrate respect for ourselves by how we dress, speak and conduct ourselves. 'Black English' is a beautiful language expression among friends and family, but Standard English should

be spoken in class. Standard English is the language of school and the workplace.

15. We will take responsibility for our own actions by recognizing that we can always change negative behavior and choices, to create positive behavior and choices.

16. We will recognize that through positive personal choices, we will not repeat critical family mistakes in the generations to follow.

17. We will truly love our people and ourselves, because we have contributed indispensable love, labor, knowledge, and sacrificed our lives to this nation and the world.

18. We will seek happiness. We deserve to enjoy the daily joys of living.

19. We will become what our purpose in life is by consistently making good choices.

20. We will educate others who are ignorant of our culture. Through education, we help eradicate racism.

21. We will compete at the highest level of skill in order to secure desired employment.

22. We will fight to secure the civil rights we enjoy today. The battle continues. It is your turn to continue to struggle for civil rights, and to treasure those rights we've attained.

23. We will seek to surround ourselves with greatness. If we don't have a father in the home, we will seek out positive adult father role models in our community, so that we may learn to be young men. If there is no mother in the home, we will surround ourselves with positive mother models in our community so that we may learn to be young women.

24. We will be great innovators. We represent the greatest musicians, dancers, singers, intellectuals, composers, etc. We will seek to be compared to

the greatness of our culture and we will not allow others to compare us to the worst of our culture, because no culture is exempt from people who represent the worst of their culture.

25. We will seek help in subjects that we find difficult, but that are absolutely essential for educational success. Everyone knows something, and no one knows everything. Seeking help demonstrates strength and not weakness. Weakness is giving up, rather than seeking help.

26. We will demonstrate discipline and respect our sexuality to avert unwanted pregnancies, sexually transmitted diseases, and emotional turmoil from engaging in behavior that requires adult maturity.

27. We will abstain from drugs, smoking, and alcohol. These items mask problems and offer only temporary relief.

28. We will respect and celebrate the intellectual accomplishments of our peers as much as we celebrate and respect the artistic accomplishments of our peers. Athletic and artistic accomplishments can be temporary, but intellectual ability lasts a lifetime, and is essential for continued self-development.

About the Author

Mary Cole Watson, M. Ed.

"I loved learning," explains Watson. Having earned the privilege to attend a catholic school not far from her home, Mary was very aware of how her learning experience was different than her white counterparts. Yet, this experience did nothing, but inspire her to rise above the bar of low expectations the Nuns set for her, and for the other children of color. Upon graduating from The College at Brockport, a state

179

university of New York, located just outside Rochester, this brave young soldier grew from being a "self-loathing burden" of the state of New York, to an award-winning teacher who instilled cultural pride in her African American students.

Born in Ansonia, Connecticut, Mary Cole Watson was the second of eleven children. Her world was often marred in chaos and confusion. Her mother suffered from an undiagnosed bout of mental illness, while her father suffered from alcoholism, like many men of color during the 1950's.

Before Mary was whisked off to spend some of her most formative years in foster care, she had already made it up in her mind that she wanted to be a teacher. As early as the age of six, she found herself challenging the minds of her younger siblings with math, reading, and language writing in their makeshift classroom. Lined up on the floor in front of their beds, she would firmly articulate the correct spelling of the word for the day to her younger brother Gerard.

Watson made it her life goal to ensure the next generation of learners understood their designated place in African American heritage. Her drive resulted in graduating Magna Cum Laude, and later the recipient of a Full Graduate Assistantship to the University of Toledo, with a Masters in Early Childhood Education and Reading.

Made in the USA
Columbia, SC
06 September 2022